If You Could Ask God One Question

Paul Williams and Barry Cooper

CHRISTIANITY EXPLORED BOOKS

This 2007 edition published by
The Good Book Company Ltd
Elm House, 37 Elm Road,
New Malden, Surrey KT3 3HB, UK
Tel: 0845 225 0880; Fax: 0845 225 0990
Tel International: (+44) 208 942 0880
Fax International: (+44) 208 942 0990
E-mail: admin@thegoodbook.co.uk
website: www.thegoodbook.co.uk

ISBN: 1–904889–45–X
ISBN 13: 978–1–904889–45–8

Cover design by Carl Hamblin and Steve Devane
Printed in the UK by CPD

For Susannah, Bethan and Joshua

Contents

Where To Begin?

"Martin," I said to my friend, "if you could ask God one question, and you knew it would be answered, what would it be?"

Martin looked serious. I could tell this was going to be something deeply felt, possibly quite emotional.

"Is Elvis *really* dead?"

I blinked.

"*That* would be your question?"

"Yes", said Martin.

Trying to be sensitive, I suggested, "It's not really a matter of life and death though, is it Martin?"

He thought for a moment.

"It is if you're Elvis."

The Bible itself is full of people asking God questions. But if *you* could ask God one question, what would it be?

Maybe you've already read the contents page of this book and spotted the question you'd most like to ask. If so, let me encourage you to read the book from start to finish, rather than jumping in at the relevant point. Very often, the answer to one question lays the foundation for one that follows.

And if it sometimes seems that I've given short shrift to a big question, let me apologise in advance and point you towards www.christianityexplored.org/onequestion where you'll find some suggestions for digging deeper. Whatever questions you want to ask God, it's my sincere hope that this book will go some way to helping you with them.

"But Paul," you might be saying, "how do we know that God even *exists*? After all, if he's really there, why on earth doesn't he prove it?"

Now *that's* a good question...

01

"If You're Really There, God, Why On Earth Don't You Prove It?"

"This morning, boys and girls, we're going to do some painting. You can paint anything you like, and if you don't know what to paint, just paint what you did at the weekend." The primary school teacher watched as the children got their plastic aprons on and started to paint enthusiastically.

After a while, the teacher walked around the room to see how they were getting on. Some were painting mummy and daddy in the park, others were painting the seaside, and some were painting the animals they'd seen at the zoo. Eventually the teacher stopped over a particularly shapeless and colourful painting.

"That's very nice, Scott," she said encouragingly, "what is it?"

"Oh, that's God," said Scott.

"But no-one's ever seen God," said the teacher.

Scott looked up at her.

"They have now."

It's not only small children who paint pictures of God. Think of the thousands of different people who've been doing just that since the dawn of time. There've been gods in the shape of animals, gods in the shape of fire or water, gods in the stars and the sun, distant gods, inner gods, benign gods and fearsome ones. And I guess if I were to ask *you* to paint a picture of God, it would probably be different to Scott's and different to mine. Perhaps you'd just leave the paper blank.

But would any of our pictures be more accurate than the imaginative doodlings of a small child? The only way we'd know is if God decided to reveal himself unmistakably, once and for all.

Steve joined the staff of the newspaper I worked for, and we used to talk all the way through lunch about the important things in life. And then, when we stopped talking about football, the conversation sometimes turned to God. "Listen," he said, "I'd believe in God if he were to come and stand in front of me. If I could meet him, talk to him and touch him. If only I could *see* him, *that* would prove his existence. *Then* I'd be convinced."

I sat there silently evaluating the odds of God suddenly appearing in the Bedfordshire Times cafeteria. (To be fair, there had been a brief visit from the Mayor recently, but having sampled the Spanish omelette, I didn't think he'd be returning in a hurry.)

But just imagine. Imagine what it would be like to physically meet God. To actually *see* him, *talk* to him, *touch* him. To actually sit down and eat with him.

Philip was another man with a similar request to Steve. I've never met Philip personally, but you can read about him in the Bible. He said to a man called Jesus, "Show me God – that's all I need."[1] And Jesus seemed surprised that Philip could ask such a thing.

"Don't you know me, Philip, even after I have been among you such a long time? *Anyone who has seen me has seen the Father.*"[2]

---

[1] John 14:8, my paraphrase. [2] John 14:9, my italics.

Yes, you read that right. Jesus is saying, once you've seen me, all the questions, all the guessing games, all the bets about what God is like – well, they're all off. Even more so than the Spanish omelette. *Anyone who has seen me has seen the Father*.

And actually, although my friend Steve can't physically touch God, or see him, or eat with him, there were many thousands of people who did just that. Many of them – wanting to keep a record of these extraordinary events – made sure to write down what happened, so that people like Steve, people like you and me, could know for certain that, yes, God does exist. As we read the Bible, these witnesses tell us again and again, "God *does* exist. And we should know. Because we met him."

But didn't they just make this stuff up? Jesus never actually claimed to be God, did he?

It's funny you should say that, because Jesus *did* claim to be God. Repeatedly. Although not always directly.

When Jesus said, for instance, "I and the Father are one",[3] he wasn't just making some vague claim to be "in tune" with God. He was actually claiming to *be* God. And if you need convincing of that, just look at the way the religious leaders reacted at the time:

> [They] picked up stones to stone him, but Jesus said to them, "I have shown you many great miracles from the Father. For which of these do you stone me?"
>
> "We are not stoning you for any of these," replied the Jews, "but for blasphemy, *because you, a mere man, claim to be God*."
>
> John 10:31–33, my italics[4]

---

[3] John 10:30. [4] John 10:31–33 means the book of John in the Bible, chapter 10, verses 31 to 33.

As you can see, they were in no doubt about what Jesus meant when he said "I and the Father are one." And Jesus makes no attempt to correct their thinking on the matter, even though they are about to try and kill him for it.

Not only does Jesus not correct them, he carries on repeating the claim, in ways that were unmistakable to the people that heard him. People who were familiar with this prophecy, for example:

> "…this is what the Sovereign LORD says: I myself will search for my sheep and look after them… I myself will tend my sheep… declares the Sovereign LORD… I will shepherd the flock with justice."   Ezekiel 34:11, 15-16

And what does Jesus say, in the light of that six hundred year-old prediction?

> "I am the good shepherd."   John 10:11, 14

In other words, I am the Sovereign Lord you've been reading about.

And that statement, "I am the good shepherd", is even more astonishing when you realise the deep significance of that simple phrase, "I am…". Those two words on the lips of Jesus are unimaginably shocking. About fifteen hundred years before Jesus walked the earth, a man called Moses was told by God that he (Moses) would lead God's people, the Israelites, out of captivity in Egypt. Moses is doubtful, and thinks the Israelites will be too. He wants some way of proving that he has indeed been talking to God himself:

> Moses said to God, "Suppose I go to the Israelites and say to them, 'The God of your fathers has sent me to you,' and they ask me, 'What is his name?' Then what shall I tell them?"

> God said to Moses, "I AM WHO I AM. This is what you are to
> say to the Israelites: 'I AM has sent me to you.'"   Exodus 3:13–14

God tells Moses his name, and his name is I AM.

Now fast forward to Jesus' time, where once again, we find Jesus talking to the religious authorities. This time they're talking about Abraham, a man who had been born some two thousand years before Jesus said the following:

> "…Your father Abraham rejoiced at the thought of seeing my day; he saw it and was glad."
>
> "You are not yet fifty years old," the Jews said to him, "and you have seen Abraham!"
>
> "I tell you the truth," Jesus answered, "before Abraham was born, *I am*!"   John 8:56–58

To even *say* God's name was something to be done with great reverence and fear, *but Jesus actually applies the name to himself*. As you might expect, the religious leaders again pick up stones and try to kill him for making this extraordinary, blasphemous claim.

And this is not – by any means – the only occasion when Jesus used that unique and telling phrase, "I am". He also said:

"I am the light of the world."	John 8:12; 9:5
"I am the bread of life."	John 6:35,48
"I am the true vine."	John 15:1
"I am the resurrection and the life."	John 11:25
"I am the way and the truth and the life."	John 14:6

These words are not only stunning, they are stunningly dangerous.

I know that if I were to say, "Why don't you support a proper football team like Leeds?" to a gang of heavily tattooed Manchester United fans, then the next thing I'd see would almost certainly be the inside of an ambulance. There are certain words, spoken in certain circumstances, that will eventually get you killed.

And yet Jesus made a habit of it. He insisted quite unashamedly that he was indeed God, the Lord of everything, Creator of heaven and earth. He even said these things while on trial for his life before the highest religious court in the land:

> Again the high priest asked him, "Are you the Christ, the Son of the Blessed One?"
>
> "I am," said Jesus. Mark 14:61–62

Anyone can *claim* to be God, though, can't they?

Absolutely. Lots of people like to talk themselves up a bit, like rap artists, or boxers at a pre-fight press conference.

Take Muhammad Ali, for example. He is one of the greatest boxers the world has ever seen, and listening to the things he said to his opponents before he even entered the ring, you suspect he won fights without throwing a single punch. "I have wrestled with an alligator! I tussled with a whale! I handcuffed lightning, threw thunder in jail! Only last week, I murdered a rock, injured a stone, hospitalized a brick. I'm so mean, I make medicine sick!" Again and again he would claim, "I am the greatest." In fact, according to Ali, there was only one thing he found hard: "When you're as great as I am, it's hard to be humble".[5]

But there was one thing Ali knew better than most: if you're going to talk about yourself in that way, you will be the laughing stock of the whole world – unless you back up the talk with action. And that is exactly what Jesus did.

---

[5] Quoted at http://mjengakenya.blogspot.com/ accessed 9th July 2007.

It is no ordinary human being who *can* actually handcuff lightning and throw thunder in jail. Let's face it, ordinary human beings can't even *predict* the weather accurately, let alone control it. But Jesus was different.

He was asleep in a boat, and his close followers (referred to as "disciples" in the Bible) were at the oars. Suddenly, a fierce storm hits the lake they're rowing across, and the boat is in danger of sinking. And this is no storm in a teacup, because it prompts the disciples – several of whom are fishermen familiar with extreme conditions – to wake Jesus with the desperate cry, "Master, Master, we're going to drown!"

What Jesus does next is astonishing:

> He got up and rebuked the wind and the raging waters; the
> storm subsided, and all was calm.   Luke 8:24

So much for the weather forecast. Jesus tells the storm to stop. And it stops. The disciples, unsurprisingly, are dumbfounded: "Who is this? He commands even the winds and the water, and they obey him."

I cannot tell you how much I'd love to have that power. I always avoid travelling by sea if I can. The worst time was when my wife and I were on a cross-channel ferry. As we drove onto the ship, the crew began to secure all the vehicles with ropes, which I have to say was not an encouraging sight. As everyone else went off to enjoy a hearty meal at the on-board restaurant, I found a seat just outside the toilets. This proved wise, because shortly afterwards I started to feel ill. Really ill. In fact, I don't think I, or anyone else, have ever been so sick.

When I could stand it no longer, I looked up at Caroline, and like a little boy on a long car journey I said in a pathetic voice, "Are we nearly there yet?"

As it happened, we hadn't even left the harbour.

What I wouldn't have given to have gone up on deck, said to the wind and waves, "Be quiet!", and have them actually obey me. It would annoy the surfers further up the beach of course, but imagine it! To have that kind of power. Only one person in all of human history has ever done anything like it.

Impressive, but it could simply have been a coincidence, couldn't it?
It could've been – if it had been an isolated incident.

People who spent any time at all around Jesus witnessed the most extraordinary things. And not just those who were on his side. People who wanted to kill him often witnessed miracles in his presence, and they never tried to deny any of them. Why? Because everyone knew that these miracles actually happened. They were beyond question. The only thing people disagreed about was *how* Jesus was able to do these things.

Things like feeding five thousand men with the contents of a small child's packed lunch. Walking on water. Effortlessly curing sickness, paralysis, blindness, deafness. Bringing the dead back to life.[6]

When Jesus walked the earth, he behaved as if he owned the place. Looking at the evidence, it's easy to see why.

Is Jesus the real thing? Couldn't he somehow trick people into thinking he was who he said he was?
It would certainly be an impressive series of tricks. If they *were* tricks, it is incredible that none of his enemies were

---

[6]If you'd like to read about these incidents, look at Mark 6:30–44; Matthew 14:22–33; Luke 4:40; Matthew 9:2–7; John 9:1–11; Mark 7:32–34; Matthew 9:18–19, 23–25; Luke 7:11–14; and John 11:38–44.

ever able to expose him as a fraud at any time during his life, or since. And, unlike con artists, it's not as if Jesus used his apparent power to gain a life of wealth, worldly status, sensual indulgence or luxury. Quite the opposite, in fact. He associated himself with the poverty-stricken, the unloved, the outcasts with contagious diseases. He welcomed children with open arms and treated women with a dignity that was unheard of at the time.

But there's another reason to believe that Jesus is the real thing. For many hundreds of years before Jesus lived, biblical writers had been predicting in detail the birth, life and death of the Christ. Some of these prophecies could conceivably have been fulfilled "wilfully" by Jesus, like the prophecy which specified Galilee as the place where most of the work of the Christ would be done.[7] But many others could not. You cannot pre-arrange your own birthplace, for example.[8] Unless you commit suicide, it's very difficult to pre-arrange the exact circumstances of your own death.[9] And it is seemingly impossible to predict (accurately) that three days after your death, you will live again – of which, more later. The fact is, Jesus perfectly fits the picture painted by hundreds of prophecies written in the Bible hundreds of years before he was born.

A few years ago a member of the Royal Family came to visit the church I was working in. Before she arrived, there were frantic preparations to make sure everything was ready for her. Junk was cleared away, walls were

---

[7] "…in the future he will honour Galilee of the Gentiles, by the way of the sea, along the Jordan…" (Isaiah 9:1)

[8] "But you, Bethlehem Ephrathah, though you are small among the clans of Judah, out of you will come for me one who will be ruler over Israel, whose origins are from of old, from ancient times." (Micah 5:2)

[9] "…a band of evil men has encircled me, they have pierced my hands and my feet. I can count all my bones; people stare and gloat over me. They divide my garments among them and cast lots for my clothing." (Psalm 22:16–18)

given a fresh coat of paint, carpets were rolled out. The last job of all – by royal command – was to fit a brand new toilet seat, which became affectionately known as The Royal Throne.

We did everything in our power to prepare for the arrival of our royal visitor, and we were pleased to do it because it was such an honour to have her among us.

A man called John the Baptist did a similar kind of thing. He was intent on preparing the way for the Christ, and announcing his arrival. He lived at the same time as Jesus, he knew all about the prophecies, and when John heard of all the amazing things that Jesus was doing, John sent his followers to ask Jesus explicitly, "Are you the one who was to come, or should we expect someone else?"[10] Jesus replied: "Go back and report to John what you hear and see: The blind receive sight, the lame walk, those who have leprosy are cured, the deaf hear, the dead are raised, and the good news is preached to the poor."[11] His words carry a deliberate and unmistakable echo of a prophecy written seven hundred years earlier:

> …say to those with fearful hearts,
>> "Be strong, do not fear;
> *your God will come…"*
> Then will the eyes of the blind be opened
>> and the ears of the deaf unstopped.
> Then will the lame leap like a deer,
>> and the mute tongue shout for joy.   Isaiah 35:4–6, my italics

Your God has come, says Jesus. All the prophecies are fulfilled in me.

---

[10] Matthew 11:2–3. [11] Matthew 11:4–5.

Now, I don't know what your background is, but it may be that you're so familiar with the miracles of Jesus, they don't have the impact they once did.

But just think about it for a moment: who can give sight to people who have been blind from birth? Who can open deaf ears, enable hopelessly paralysed people to walk, control nature, cure incurable illnesses? Who can bring corpses back to life *with a word*? Doctors? Spiritual gurus? Holistic practitioners? I have watched people die, and maybe you have too. Ultimately, there was nothing that *anyone* could do to stop them dying, and the inevitability of our own death proves the same sorry fact. There are some things that are simply beyond our capacity as human beings.

So what Jesus did – repeatedly and effortlessly – was truly superhuman. He demonstrated, beyond reasonable doubt, that he is more than just a man. However staggering the implications, Jesus' words and actions graphically prove that he *is* God.

As we sat in the cafeteria of the Bedfordshire Times, my friend Steve wanted proof of God's existence: "If you're really there, God, why on earth don't you prove it?"

It seems to me that when Jesus walked the planet, God did, on earth, prove it.

02

"Isn't The Bible Just A Bunch Of Made-Up Stories?"

Or, as we say in French, "Est-ce que la Bible jusq'un bunch de stories fabriqué?"

Yes, that's right. I failed even basic French at school. Even now, I'm useless on vacation unless circumstances require me to retrieve a condiment ("Où est le sel, mademoiselle?") or state the current position of a family pet ("Le hamster est dans le jardin").

However, I do remember one vital thing from my French lessons: the importance of accents. Not the accent you use when you speak, but the accents you place over letters when you write. There are five main ones in French, apparently. One looks like this: ˆ . Another looks like this: ´. The third looks like this: ` . And so on.

They're not much to look at are they? Sneeze while you're reading this page, and you might have a hard time finding them again. They're no more than a brief stroke of the pen. But if that brief stroke of a pen happens to be written in the Bible, says Jesus, it takes on enormous and lasting significance:

> "I tell you the truth, until heaven and earth disappear, not the smallest letter, nor the least stroke of a pen, will by any means disappear from the Law [what we call the "Old Testament"] until everything is accomplished."   Matthew 5:18

As far as Jesus is concerned, even the tiniest mark on the page of the Old Testament[1] holds unique power. According to him, whether you call it "the Law", "Scripture" or the "Old Testament", one thing holds true: it comes from God, and its authority is unquestionable. "Scripture cannot be broken", he says in John chapter 10 verse 35.

And why is Jesus' view of Scripture so important?
Some opinions are worth more than others. Take Thomas Andrews, creator of the doomed ship, Titanic. According to the opinion of some – even after it struck an iceberg – the ship was "unsinkable". But following an inspection of the damage done, Andrews knew that Titanic would sink within "an hour and a half… possibly two. Not much longer."[2]

Passengers were instructed to get in to the lifeboats, women and children first. "Ladies you must get in at once!" he cried, moving among the boats. Some thought that the danger was being exaggerated. Andrews came across two women joking that one boat looked prettier than another, and he spoke more firmly: "You cannot pick and choose your boat! Don't hesitate, get in at once! Get in!"

You can imagine the ladies' laughter evaporating fairly quickly when he said that. Those words, spoken by a man of his authority – the creator of the ship, no less – carried tremendous weight.

As we saw in the last chapter, Jesus' words – which could calm storms, cure disease, faultlessly predict the

---

[1] The Old Testament was written before Jesus was born; the New Testament was written after, and begins at the book of Matthew.
[2] Quoted at http://www.geocities.com/Athens/Aegean/6136/impossible.html accessed 9th July 2007.

future and cause the dead to live again – carry more authority than the words of anyone who has ever lived. His words, as we can see from the miraculous effect they had, demonstrate that he really is the ultimate authority. He is the Creator of the universe, no less – and his words carry tremendous weight.

But Jesus never questioned the authority of the Old Testament. On the contrary, he considered it so authoritative that he used it to demolish the arguments of his opponents by simply drawing their attention to the tense of a particular verb contained within it. For example, when he was debating with the Sadducees – a religious group who did not believe in life after death – Jesus said this:

> "Now about the dead rising – have you not read in the book of Moses, in the account of the bush, how God said to him, 'I *am* the God of Abraham, the God of Isaac, and the God of Jacob'? He is not the God of the dead, but of the living. You are badly mistaken!"
> Mark 12:26–27, my italics

The Sadducees didn't have any comeback for that one. When God spoke to Moses, these men Abraham, Isaac and Jacob had been dead for years, and yet God said very clearly, I *am* their God. He didn't say, I *was* their God. Therefore, says Jesus, there very clearly *is* life after death! All of which might seem a bit academic to you, but it shows how unanswerable the Old Testament is as far as Jesus is concerned. Over and over again, Jesus quoted the Old Testament to expose the wrong-thinking of the religious establishment.

Jesus also treated the Bible's history as completely reliable, right from its very first page. He affirmed that we – and the world we live in – did not just develop out of nowhere; we are the creation of a Creator.[3] He spoke about Noah[4] as a real person who actually existed, the ark as a real ship that was actually built, and the flood as a real event that actually happened.[5] And so on.

Far from being _full_ of errors, Jesus insisted that the Bible is the only way to keep ourselves _from_ error. "Are you not in error," he says to the religious leaders, "because you do not know the Scriptures or the power of God?"[6]

So Jesus trusted the Old Testament. Why should I trust the New Testament?

My brother David has a reputation for telling stories. When he and his wife were at our house recently he began telling the story about the time I had my hair permed.

Now, as I write this, I want you to know that I feel only shame about the perm. I was weak and vulnerable, and they were on special offer. But in my defence, the story David told was almost unrecognisable from true history. About the only part of his story that was accurate was the fact that at one stage of my life I had really fuzzy hair.

All the way through the story I was chipping in with, "No, that's not true", "I never said that", "No, that's not what happened", "I did not make the barber weep", and so on.

Now, I'm not saying that everything David said was unreliable. But I am saying that, over time, this story

---

[3] "Haven't you read…that at the beginning the Creator 'made them male and female'…?" (Matthew 19:4)

[4] You can read about Noah and these events in Genesis (the first book of the Bible) chapters 6 to 9.

[5] "For in the days before the flood, people were eating and drinking, marrying and giving in marriage, up to the day Noah entered the ark…" (Matthew 24:38)

[6] Mark 12:24.

about me had slowly and subtly strayed from strict historical accuracy.

And people sometimes think that the same thing has happened with all the New Testament stories about Jesus Christ. Yes, there was a man called Jesus who really walked this planet. Yes, he was clearly a great teacher and a genuinely memorable character. But so loved was he by those closest to him that their stories about him strayed further and further from the truth until, finally, what they wrote down involved a lot of – shall we say – "colourful" incidents that couldn't possibly be accepted by any sensible human being.

If that's what you've been led to believe, it's worth hearing what Jesus has to say about the New Testament. According to him, God himself made sure of what was written in it:

> "The Holy Spirit, whom the Father will send in my name, will teach you all things and will remind you of everything I have said to you."
>
> John 14:26

> "[W]hen he, the Spirit of truth, comes, he will guide you into all truth."
>
> John 16:13

Those are very important promises. Jesus promised his disciples that after he was gone, the Spirit of God would remind them of Jesus' words and lead them into "all truth" as they wrote the New Testament. So not only would they be reminded of specific incidents, but also of specific words Jesus spoke to them.

Humanly speaking, the writers took tremendous pains over what they wrote. Let me give one example. About 25% of what we call the New Testament was written by a learned, professional man called Luke. He explains that he has only included facts that have been "handed down... by those who from the first were eye-witnesses."[7] In other words, it's not hearsay. It's the first-hand testimony of those who were actually there.

Not content simply to accept the "facts" of others, Luke also verified the information himself, just to make sure:

> I myself have carefully investigated everything... so that you may know the certainty of the things you have been taught.
>
> Luke 1:3-4

If he'd heard my brother's story, this is the kind of man who would surely have hunted down and interrogated the relevant hairdresser to get his version of events. That's what Luke did, comparing and investigating so that what he wrote down could be fully relied upon. It's not as if most of the key players in the story were no longer around to verify what was being claimed: the New Testament was written within the lifetimes of those who first witnessed the events that are recorded.

And it's not as if these events took place "in a corner",[8] as another New Testament writer, Paul, points out. This was history played out on a grand scale, in the middle of towns, villages, cities. Take for example one of the most important events recorded in the New Testament: Jesus' resurrection from death. Paul mentions witnesses who saw Jesus alive *after* his public execution, and the list includes this staggering statement:

> After that, [Jesus] appeared to *more than five hundred* of the brothers at the same time, *most of whom are still living*, though some have fallen asleep [i.e. died].   1 Corinthians 15:6, my italics

---

[7] Luke 1:2. [8] Acts 26:26.

After Jesus rose from the dead, he appeared to more than five hundred people, most of whom were still alive at the time of writing. Paul is saying to his contemporaries: "Don't believe me? Most of the witnesses are still alive – hop on a camel and go talk to them. Find out for yourself."

You see, my brother can say what he likes about my perm, but many of his claims could easily be disproved by talking to trustworthy people who were around at the time. Witnesses to my hair, if you like. Was my hair really as big as Leo Sayer's? Did I really look like Michael Jackson when he was fronting the Jackson Five? Well, let's talk to the people who knew me at the time and find out. After all, if their stories don't match up with my brother's, then we'd be right to question his claims, wouldn't we?

Bedtime in the Williams household is quite an event. It follows immediately after Bathtime, during which our three children, Joshua (the youngest, aged 2), Susannah and Bethan (twins, aged 5) have absolutely drenched their daddy (grown man who really should know better, 43). After Bathtime, we settle down for Storytime. Over the last four years, I have read so many children's stories I can recite many of them with my eyes closed, word perfect, and with the uncanny ability to predict exactly what the children will say as I turn each page. And one thing you can usually rely on is that most fairy stories begin in a similar way: "Once upon a time, in a land far away..."

Once... at a time we can't determine... in a place of uncertain geographical location... that's the land of fairy stories for you. But take even a brief look at what Luke writes, and you'll see that his book is no fairy tale. Chapter 2, for example, tells us of Jesus' birth. It does not begin, "Once upon a time..." It starts like this:

> In those days Caesar Augustus issued a decree that a census should be taken of the entire Roman world. (This was the first census that took place while Quirinius was governor of Syria.)
>
> Luke 2:1–2

These events do not take place "in a land far away", but in a world very much our own, albeit the world as it was two thousand years ago. It's not "once upon a time", but when "the first census that took place while Quirinius was Governor of Syria." And none of this happens "in a land far away," but in the "Roman world." This is not the world you find in fairy tales, but the world you find in history books. The writers of the New Testament (and the Old) write with the assurance and conviction of men who are writing about real events that actually happened. They are not fabricating fond tales from the depths of their own imaginations.[9]

So you're saying that God himself made sure the Bible can be trusted?

If God is there, isn't it reasonable to suppose that he could have done such a thing, if he wanted? And if he *had* done such a thing, you'd expect the Bible to be quite unlike any other book. It is.

Despite the fact that it contains sixty-six different books, written by dozens of different writers, most of whom never met each other, over a period of one thousand five hundred years, the Bible has a *single unifying* theme. Time and again, archaeological discoveries have supported the history within it.[10]

---

[9] "We did not follow cleverly invented stories when we told you about the power and coming of our Lord Jesus Christ, but we were eye-witnesses of his majesty." (2 Peter 1:16)

[10] To read more about the archaeological evidence, visit www.christianityexplored.org/onequestion.

It makes literally hundreds of remarkable predictions that are then demonstrably fulfilled years later. More than three hundred of these are fulfilled by Jesus himself.[11]

What's more, if you choose to take the Bible at its word, you will discover for yourself that it is not the ill-remembered writings of men long since dead and buried. You will discover that the Bible is the divinely powerful Word of God, with the authority to transform lives radically, even here, at the start of the twenty-first century. To those who doubted his words, Jesus lays down this challenge:

> "If anyone chooses to do God's will, he will find out whether
> my teaching comes from God or whether I speak on my own."
>
> John 7:17

In other words, if you want to know – subjectively, in your own experience – that the Bible really *is* God's word, you can. Because when you put its teaching into practice, the miraculous results in your own life are such that you will *know* the words could only have come from God.

But you'll have to take *my* word for that. Unless of course…

---

[11] See the previous chapter for some examples of prophecies that Jesus fulfilled.

03

"All Good People Go To Heaven, Right?"

You've probably gathered by now that I was not a child of great academic promise. But sports were different, because for some reason I have always had pretty good hand-eye coordination.

Replace my French dictionary with a badminton racket ("la raquette badminton"), and I am transformed. I loved badminton so much I used to play my dad every weekend. And eventually, my passion began to pay off. I found I could beat most of the other kids in my year at school.

My friend Lawrence suggested I sign up for a tournament that he would be playing in and, the night before it started, I was already having visions of the grand final: a dramatic yet crowd-pleasing triumph against Lawrence. I'd even begun to work on the victory speech. Perhaps I would clamber into the stands for a tearful embrace with my proud parents. In the post-match interview, I could hear Lawrence saying, "I played my best badminton out there today, but Williams was just too strong for me."

The next day, I played three boys in the qualifying stages and was thrashed by all three. Played off the court. To make matters worse, none of the kids who beat me got much further in the competition. A competition that was won by: my friend Lawrence. Convincingly.

Several uncomfortable lessons were learnt that day, but this was the one that struck me hardest: _how good we think we are depends on who we compare ourselves to_.

In Mark chapter 10, someone else learns a similar lesson:

> As Jesus started on his way, a man ran up to him and fell on his knees before him. "Good teacher," he asked, "what must I do to inherit eternal life?"
>
> "Why do you call me good?" Jesus answered. "No-one is good – except God alone." Mark 10:17–18

The man wants to know how to get to heaven. And he assumes that there is something he can "do" to get there, that somehow, by doing enough good things, he can be good enough for God. "Good teacher," he says, "what must I do to inherit eternal life?"

Jesus immediately picks up on that word, "good": he makes the startling statement that "_no-one_ is good – except God alone."

"No-one is good"? I know lots of good people. Surely Jesus isn't saying that _they_ aren't good?
It's certainly an outrageous claim.

And that's why, at this point, Jesus encourages the man to compare his own goodness with the goodness of God. After all, _how good people think they are depends on who they compare themselves to_.

Jesus does this by turning the man's attention to the ten commandments, the true guide as to what is truly good, the laws given by God himself which reflect the "goodness" of God's character:

> "You know the commandments: 'Do not murder, do not commit adultery, do not steal, do not give false testimony, do not defraud, honour your father and mother.'"
>
> "Teacher," he declared, "all these I have kept since I was a boy." Mark 10:19–20

The man thinks of himself as a good person, certainly good enough to go to heaven. There are many religious and moral achievements on his CV. He is convinced that he's kept the commandments Jesus mentions.

But you may have noticed something odd about Jesus' list of the ten commandments. There aren't ten of them.

In fact, he deliberately and conspicuously leaves out some of the ten in order to focus the man's attention on them.

There's no mention, for example, of the very first commandment, "You shall have no other gods before me." Or, for that matter, the second: "You shall not make for yourself an idol." Jesus tries to focus the man's attention on these commandments because – whether he realises it or not – the man has been breaking them all his life.

As a matter of fact, he's about to break them once again:

> Jesus looked at him and loved him. "One thing you lack," he said. "Go, sell everything you have and give to the poor, and you will have treasure in heaven. Then come, follow me."
>
> At this the man's face fell. He went away sad, because he had great wealth. Mark 10:21–22

Patiently and lovingly, Jesus is showing the man that there are some commandments he has *not* kept. "You shall have no other gods before me" – and yet the man's wealth has become a god to him. "You shall not make for yourself an idol" – and yet the money he has made has become something he worships. If those things were not true, the man would gladly have done what Jesus tells him to do. But instead, he walks away.

Compared with other people, the man probably thought he *was* good enough to get to heaven. But compared with the moral perfection, the blazing purity of God himself?

The question is: what would we have done if we were in the man's position? What is the one thing that would make us walk away from the "treasure in heaven" Jesus offers, if only we will follow him?

Of course, it may not be money that is the issue for us. We might walk away from Jesus for a very different reason. Maybe because our career is more important to us, or because a particular relationship is more important to us, or because our sense of our own goodness is more important to us. Can we really claim to be good – can we really claim that we deserve heaven – if we would rather put those things at the centre of our lives, rather than the loving God who made us, and gives us every good thing we enjoy?

Are you saying that I have to give away all my money to get to heaven?

It's important to notice what Jesus does *not* say. He does not say that people go to heaven because they give to the poor. Lots of people give to the poor, but never give a second thought to God.

And that's the heart of the problem, according to Jesus. We *all* put other things before God. We all walk away from God because we love other things more than him. If we loved him as we should, if the joy of knowing him satisfied us more than *anything* else in the world, then it would be easy for us to sell everything we have and give to the poor. We could do it as easily and unbegrudgingly as a man who owns the Atlantic would give away a small cup of salty water.

But we don't. Because we love *things* much more than the God who created them, and gave them to us. This rich man certainly did: "At this the man's face fell. He went away sad, because he had great wealth." Jesus challenges him to choose between God and money, and, as he walks away, it's clear where the man's loyalties lie. This is the moment when the man reveals two things about himself: how far he is from good, and how far he is from God. For all of his religious and moral "goodness", the "one thing" the man lacks is love for God.

And isn't it tragic that he walks away "sad"? It's a terrible irony that the wealth he clings to cannot stop him feeling discontented. The very thing he is putting in place of God has no lasting power to satisfy him and, of course, it can never give him the one thing he craves more than anything else: "eternal life".

As a young boy, I imagined that to be the best tennis player in the world would make me perfectly fulfilled. So I spent hours practising, whacking tennis balls against the garage door, the incessant thud, thud, thud driving my parents to distraction. I remember watching John McEnroe play at Wimbledon when I was a teenager, and imagining how satisfying it would be to be *that* good at something. It seemed to me the ultimate dream.

When I was a little older, I read John McEnroe's autobiography, *Serious*. What I imagined as heaven on earth – being Wimbledon Champion and number one in the world – he describes like this:

On October 1, 1984, I was standing in the Portland airport, waiting to board a flight to LA for a week off, and suddenly I thought, I'm the greatest tennis player who ever lived – why am I so empty inside? Except for the French, and one tournament just before the Open in which I had been basically over-tennised, I won every tournament I played in 1984: thirteen out of fifteen. Eighty-two out of eighty-five matches. No-one had ever had a year like that in tennis before. No-one has since. It wasn't enough. The feeling had been building up for a while. I'd been number one for four years, and I never felt especially happy.[1]

Although we may not feel it as acutely as John McEnroe (in fact, we may feel perfectly happy as we are), we can only have the things we need most deeply – certainty of heaven in the face of death, forgiveness, contentment – when we do what the rich man could not do: put Jesus first. Love God more than anything else. And we will only do that when we realise how much we need him.

Remember what Jesus said when the man called him "good teacher"? He said, "Why do you call me good? No-one is good – except God alone." Ironically, although the man was wrong about his own goodness, he was right about the goodness of Jesus. No-one has ever been truly "good" in the way that Jesus was good. Anyone who reads one of the four accounts of Jesus' life[2] can see for themselves what goodness really is: here was a man who kept all the commandments perfectly, a man who was always kind, always compassionate, always courageous; who spent his time with those no-one else could bring themselves to love; who gave up his life for those who despised him. Not even his enemies found a trace of

---

[1] John McEnroe, *Serious* (Time Warner Paperbacks, 2003).
[2] The books of the Bible called Matthew, Mark, Luke and John.

hypocrisy in him. *That's* how good we need to be for heaven. And only one person has ever managed it. No-one is that good, except God alone.

But what's so bad about "not being good enough"?

It's not as if God is like some strict headmaster, shaking his head in disappointment at the shoddy grades of his pupils, or a pushy parent with unrealistically high hopes for their children. It's not that we "don't quite live up to" the unattainable standards of our Creator. What we've done to God is much more serious than that. Let me explain.

The Bedfordshire Times may not seem to you like a hotbed of seething ambition, but like many a guy in his twenties, I wanted to climb the corporate ladder. In this case, the next rung on the ladder was my boss's. I used to dream about having his job, his company BMW and his office. Especially his office. It was absolutely huge, with huge paintings lining the walls, a huge desk (complete with one of those fiddly executive toys with silver metal balls that go click-click-click against one another like a Geiger counter gone mad) and, best of all, a huge leather swivel-chair. I could imagine "PAUL WILLIAMS, SALES AND PROMOTIONS MANAGER" sitting in that magnificent chair, giving orders into the intercom like some crazed general in his war-time bunker.

Not that I would've shared this dream with my boss. He was a deeply scary man who took no nonsense from any of us, and he would quite rightly be livid if he thought I had designs on his job. We were all terrified of him.

But one evening, I had to put a report on the boss's vast, inviting desk so that it would be ready for him first thing in the morning. As I walked into his office, it suddenly occurred to me that everyone apart from the cleaners had gone home. So I did what anyone else would've done: I slid into the plush leather upholstery and took it for a test drive. Then, after one or two spins in the swivel-chair, I decided to swing my legs up onto the desk and recline, like a panther after a particularly satisfying kill. I then decided to pick up the boss's phone and call a friend, just so that I could say, "Guess where I'm sitting right now?"

And at that precise moment, the boss walked in.

I remember there was a brief pause as two pairs of eyes wondered whether they were really seeing what they thought they were seeing. I also remember both of us turning an unexpectedly hot shade of red, but for different reasons.

I was first to speak.

"Why aren't you at home?"

I know. In hindsight, I was probably not in a position to be asking *him* questions.

But *that* is a tiny glimpse of what you and I have done to God. Regardless of whether or not we live our lives by a strict moral code, regardless of the fact that we can always find others to compare ourselves favourably with, all of us – all of us – put ourselves in the place that rightly belongs to God. Or, like the wealthy man we've just been reading about, we put *things* in the place of God: cash, career, sex, status, self-esteem, family, fame, popularity, power, our own moral superiority, or whatever it is that calls the shots in our lives. Living in this way is what the Bible calls "sin".

And if putting myself in the boss's chair is a serious thing to do to the manager of the Bedfordshire Times, you can begin to imagine how serious it is when we do it to the Creator of the universe, the very one who has given us our lives, and grants us every last breath we draw.

As Jesus says, we owe God everything: "Love the Lord your God with all your heart and with all your soul and with all your mind. This is the first and greatest commandment."[3] But my heart has been busy doing other things, as Jesus points out:

> "...from within, out of men's hearts, come evil thoughts, sexual immorality, theft, murder, adultery, greed, malice, deceit, lewdness, envy, slander, arrogance and folly. All these evils come from inside and make an man 'unclean.'"
>
> Mark 7:21–23

In other words, none of us is good. That list alone is enough to condemn every one of us.

But most devastating of all is the *order* of the list. If Jesus had started with murder or theft or adultery, many of us – like the rich man – would be saying to ourselves, "I've not done any of those things." But he doesn't; *he starts with our thoughts.* When it comes to our thoughts, says Jesus, we're all guilty. And if you doubt that, imagine what would it be like if every single one of your most private, innermost *thoughts* were loudly and publicly announced as soon as they came into your mind? What kind of words would be broadcast to the world as a work colleague makes a joke at your expense, as you surf the internet, as a person near you on the train talks loudly into their phone, as your eyes follow someone attractive as they walk past you on the street?

These thoughts *matter*, according to Jesus. Because evil doesn't just come out of nowhere. It lives in every human

---

[3] Matthew 22:36–38.

heart, regardless of whether we act on it or not. And if we're tempted to think that we are good people because we never *act* on our bad thoughts, it's worth wondering: what kinds of things would we do if we knew there would be no negative consequences for us? How many times have we been kept from doing something we wanted to do only because we were afraid that God or society or the law would punish us, or because our friends would think of us as bad people? How often do we do "the right thing" not because we love to do it, but simply because we don't want to be seen doing "the wrong thing"?

Because God is *infinitely* worthy of our love, our rejection of him – this "sin" that is so deeply ingrained in every human heart – is *infinitely* horrifying. Despite his goodness to us, we have deliberately dedicated our whole lives to putting ourselves, or other things, in his rightful place.

We don't find this easy to hear. When my boss found me lounging around in his office, my immediate instinct was to try and justify myself by demanding answers *from him*. It was absurd, really. At the very least, I needed to tell my boss that I was genuinely sorry. And then I needed to get out of his chair, and let him sit in his rightful place.

It's strange when you think about it. We don't want God ruling our lives. We want him out of the way so that we can have his job. But we want and expect to be in heaven when we die. And at the end of our lives, when the boss turns up – perhaps unexpectedly – we will have nothing to say to him in our defence.

04

"If You're A God Of Love, Why Send Anyone To Hell?"

It seems there are certain things you just can't say.

For example, in one school I read about recently, a story entitled *The Friendly Dolphin* was rejected because it "discriminates against pupils who do not live near the sea". Another story, the subversive-sounding *A Perfect Day for Ice Cream*, apparently had to be re-written without any mention of ice cream because certain schools had banned junk food. As if that were not enough, Mickey Mouse is no longer popular with authorities because he is a "scary rodent who might upset pupils", and Harry Potter has fallen out of favour because he's an orphan ("potentially upsetting").

I suspect that Jesus' words about hell would also be absent from the school reading list. And although some have tried, it would be very hard to rewrite the Gospels[1] without any mention of hell because Jesus, whose life was nothing if not loving, mentions it again and again. In fact, the word is mentioned twelve times in the Gospels, and that doesn't take into account the uncomfortable references to "eternal punishment," "eternal fire," "the fiery furnace" and "the darkness where there will be weeping and gnashing of teeth."

---

[1] The four accounts of Jesus' life in the Bible: Matthew, Mark, Luke and John.

But although these words were on the lips of Jesus frequently, he did not take them lightly. When he spoke of hell, he spoke of it in earnest as a real place; a place to be avoided at all costs; a place set aside for those who have lived their lives in rebellion against their Creator. And when Jesus talks about judgement, his words are not sneering, malicious or bloodthirsty. They are choked with tears.

I remember one occasion when I was watching the news with some friends. During one of the reports, a senior churchman from another country said, "Margaret Thatcher can go to hell." I don't think I'd have remembered his comment were it not for the reaction of one of my friends. Looking sad and deeply troubled, he said in a softly-spoken voice, "No Christian should ever wish that upon anyone."

A story told by Jesus in Luke's Gospel helps to explain why.

> "There was a rich man who was dressed in purple and fine linen and lived in luxury every day. At his gate was laid a beggar named Lazarus, covered with sores and longing to eat what fell from the rich man's table. Even the dogs came and licked his sores." Luke 16:19–21

It's a distressing contrast: the rich man lives in luxury while the beggar sits in squalor. The dogs get more from Lazarus than he does from the rich man. But that's not the most distressing part of what Jesus says.

We learn that the two men die, and while Lazarus goes to heaven, the rich man's destination is very different. And, if we have even an ounce of sensitivity, what Jesus says next will profoundly disturb us. According to Jesus, the rich man is now "in torment". The man himself says, "I am in agony in this fire."

We're also told that there is no escape from this desperate place: "those who want to go from here... cannot". Unsurprisingly, the rich man pleads for his family who are still alive, that someone would "warn them, so that they will not also come to this place of torment."

One of my biggest fears is that something terrible might happen to my children. I guess all parents feel the same, because no parent – however vigilant and however loving – can be certain of keeping their children absolutely safe at all times. There'll be times I won't be there, times when even if I *were* there I'd be powerless to protect them, and times when the tireless ingenuity of children's minds will still manage to invent some way of hurting themselves *regardless* of my being there.

But there is one loving thing I *can* do: I can warn them. Tell them the truth about playing in the road, or sticking forks in the toaster, or drinking disinfectant. I can warn them; you'd think I was uncaring if I didn't. And I hope with all my heart that they'll listen.

That's why Jesus speaks as he does about hell. He is warning people of a clear and present danger. The language he uses is uncompromising and sometimes graphic, but isn't that often how we speak when we really want our children to hear us? I don't want to make the dangers of life sound worse than they really are – believe me I take no pleasure in scaring small children – but when the danger *is* serious, when it is a matter of life or death, I will speak plainly. That's how Jesus speaks when he speaks of hell.

For example, listen to his words in Matthew chapter 5:

> "If your right eye causes you to sin, gouge it out and throw it away. It is better for you to lose one part of your body than for

your whole body to be thrown into hell. And if your right hand causes you to sin, cut it off and throw it away. It is better for you to lose one part of your body than for your whole body to go into hell."

Matthew 5:29–30

It is love that prompts Jesus to talk like this, not madness, or malice. In fact, it would be unloving if he did *not* speak like this – if, as Jesus says, hell is a reality. And by using these provocative, shocking words, Jesus intends us to listen, and take decisive measures to avoid it.[2]

But why would a God of love send anyone to hell?

Most people like to think that "God is love". Even if they've never read the Bible before, they are able to quote those three words.[3] It is a wonderful truth, full of reassurance and comfort.

But that statement – "God is love" – doesn't mean that God loves everything.

For example, God doesn't love pride. He doesn't love cruelty. He doesn't love injustice or murder. He doesn't love lying. In fact, he hates these things:

You are not a God who takes pleasure in evil;
　　with you the wicked cannot dwell.
The arrogant cannot stand in your presence;
　　you hate all who do wrong.
You destroy those who tell lies;
　　bloodthirsty and deceitful men the LORD abhors.

Psalm 5:4–6

So, strange though it may sound, hell is a loving necessity. It is the place in which evil will be locked up, once and for all.

---

[2] It's important to realise that Jesus is not arguing for literal self-mutilation here. He is using strong language in order to stress the need to deal drastically with sin.
[3] You can find the phrase twice in 1 John 4.

In the Gospel of Matthew, for example, Jesus describes hell as the place "prepared for the devil and his angels."[4]

In other words, *God created hell to deal with evil*. He made it to be the final, inescapable prison in which all evil, all rebellion against God, will be confined, never again to exert its poisonous influence. Given all the evil in the world, isn't it a tremendous reassurance to know that it does not go unnoticed by God? It is precisely *because* he's a God of love that there is a place called hell. Because of his love, he will not ignore or overlook evil. And the Bible assures us that all human sin – however trifling it may seem to us – will ultimately be judged by a God who will perfectly weigh the motives of every single human heart, and then punish accordingly, with unquestionably perfect justice. That means that we can trust God to make a fair judgement.

Even with our imperfect sense of justice, we still understand this: the greater the crime, the greater the punishment. A crime that is infinitely great deserves an infinite punishment. And even a great crime such as murder can be made even greater depending on the victim: killing a citizen is bad enough, but killing the king? We call that high treason, and reserve an even greater punishment for it. It's even more despicable if we see that that the murder weapon was a gift given by the king himself.

Hell only seems harsh when we don't see how infinitely serious it is to rebel against God. And it only seems harsh when we don't realise how infinitely *holy* God is; in other words, how entirely perfect, how completely true, how utterly good and how profoundly

---

[4] Matthew 25:41.

beautiful God is. He is infinitely worthy of our love; and we love anyone, any*thing*, but him. He gives and sustains life; and we spend it trying to wish him out of existence.

The way Jesus describes hell – and the excruciating lengths to which he went in order that people might be kept from it[5] – should prove one thing, if nothing else: God's holiness and our sin must both be infinitely great.

In fact, once we glimpse the infinite depths of human sin, and the infinite heights of God's holiness, our question may well change. Rather than demanding, "Why send anyone to hell?", we may well ask, "How can you admit anyone to heaven?"

---

[5] More on this in the next chapter.

05

"If Jesus Really Was Your Son, How Come He Got Killed?"

Heat and expectancy filled the morning air. People murmured quietly from hidden doorways, joined the babbling streams coursing down secret alleys, and finally gave themselves up to the muscular tide that careened over palm-strewn cobbles, reared up at the city gates, and surged on towards the old hill.

At the hill's summit, a naked human form is being nailed hand and foot to an elongated wooden cross. It is impossible to make out his features, because they are marred by a blackened tangle of bruising, blood and bone. As the cross is lifted up into position, a voice breaks out from the crowd that stands around it.

"Come down from the cross and save yourself!"

Muffled laughter ripples through the crowd. The soldiers continue to squabble over the man's clothes.

The patient hours pass, waiting for death to come.

A religious leader lifts his arm to point at the dying man. "He saved others, and he can't save himself!"

But then the whole crowd watch in wordless terror as the birds fall silent, and, for three whole hours, the sun gives up its place in the sky.

On that dark Friday afternoon, it must have seemed that all the remarkable claims Jesus made were worth considerably less than the wood he was nailed to. After the claims, the promises, the signs and wonders, what? A slow and agonising death shared with criminals; the unmistakable sign that God wants nothing to do with you. "THIS IS JESUS, THE KING OF THE JEWS".[1] That was the bald inscription, scratched into splintered wood, dripping irony just above his head. I doubt anyone has ever seen a king look less royal.

It's astonishing to think that the question posed by this chapter hung in the air even as Jesus hung on the cross. The Bible contains several of the taunts flung at him. "Come down from the cross, if you are the Son of God!"[2] "He's the King of Israel! Let him come down now from the cross, and we will believe in him. He trusts in God. Let God rescue him now if he wants him, for he said, 'I am the Son of God.'"[3] One of the criminals executed with him even cries out pointedly: "Aren't you the Christ? Save yourself and us!"[4]

But he didn't come down. He wasn't rescued. And for some, even today, that is enough to make them reject him.

I suppose there are really only two possibilities when we consider what happened to Jesus: he didn't save himself either because he was unable to, or because he chose not to. Which you believe depends on who you think Jesus is. In chapter 1, we explored the evidence that Jesus is God. If that statement is true, then the Creator of the whole universe was being killed that day, and indeed that is exactly what Peter (one of Jesus' closest followers) says: "You killed the author of life …"[5]

Can we really believe that "the author of life" was incapable of rescuing himself from death? Jesus himself had no such doubts. When, for example, Peter drew a

---

[1] Matthew 27:37. [2] Matthew 27:40. [3] Matthew 27:42–43. [4] Luke 23:39. [5] Acts 3:15.

sword and attacked one of those trying to arrest Jesus, Jesus stopped him:

> "Put your sword back in its place," Jesus said to him, "for all who draw the sword will die by the sword. Do you think I cannot call on my Father, and he will at once put at my disposal more than twelve legions of angels? But how then would the Scriptures be fulfilled that say it must happen in this way?"
>
> Matthew 26:52-54

At that time a legion apparently consisted of between 3,000 and 6,000 men. As you know, numbers weren't my strong suit at school, but my calculator tells me that twelve legions of angels equals between thirty-six and seventy-two *thousand* angels. Jesus is talking about an unimaginably powerful force at his disposal. Next to that kind of firepower, Peter's sword looks a bit pathetic, doesn't it?

According to Jesus, it's not that he lacks the *ability* to escape. He deliberately chose not to.

Doesn't that sound like a rather convenient excuse?

Well, take a look at Luke chapter 4, verses 28 to 30, where we read that a mob of people try to kill Jesus by taking him up to the brow of a cliff to throw him over the edge. Despite the determination of a furious crowd, Jesus simply "walked right through the crowd and went on his way."

Again, in John chapter 10 verse 39, the religious authorities want to grab Jesus and stone him to death for blasphemy, and yet we read: "Again they tried to seize him, but he escaped their grasp."

And in chapter 7, verse 30, John tells us that they "tried to seize him, but no-one laid a hand on him, because his time had not yet come."

The key to understanding why "the author of life" could have been killed lies in that last phrase, *his time had not yet come*.

Yes, Jesus had the power to escape harm at any time and in any circumstance. But there would come a right time to suffer, a right time – and a right reason – for him to die. Unlike the death that you and I must face, it was not unavoidable for Jesus. And it didn't come unexpectedly to him. Nor was it an accident.

It was a choice:

> From that time on Jesus began to explain to his disciples that he must go to Jerusalem and suffer many things at the hands of the elders, chief priests and teacher of the law, and that he must be killed...
> Matthew 16:21

Jesus deliberately chose to go to Jerusalem, knowing that his enemies awaited him there, eager to have him killed. Not long after that, when they met together in the region called Galilee, Jesus reminded them:

> "The Son of Man is going to be betrayed into the hands of men. They will kill him..."
> Matthew 17:22–23

Again, as he was going to Jerusalem with the disciples, he told them in no uncertain terms:

> "We are going up to Jerusalem, and the Son of Man will be betrayed to the chief priests and the teachers of the law. They will condemn him to death and will turn him over to the Gentiles to be mocked and flogged and crucified."
> Matthew 20:17–19

It was a choice. And, unlike you and I, Jesus is able to predict exactly how and when he would die.

In fact, the circumstances of his death were predicted

in detail hundreds of years before they came to pass. Before his trial, before his arrest, even before he was born. We read about it in a book called Psalms, written years before the Roman concept of crucifixion had even been invented:

> All who see me mock me;
>> they hurl insults, shaking their heads:
>
> "He trusts in the LORD;
>> let the LORD rescue him.
>
> Let him deliver him,
>> since he delights in him."
>
> … I am poured out like water,
>> and all my bones are out of joint.
>
> My heart has turned to wax;
>> it has melted away within me.
>
> My strength is dried up like a potsherd,
>> and my tongue sticks to the roof of my mouth;
>> you lay me in the dust of death.
>
> Dogs have surrounded me;
>> a band of evil men has encircled me,
>> they have pierced my hands and my feet.
>
> I can count all my bones;
>> people stare and gloat over me.
>
> They divide my garments among them
>> and cast lots for my clothing.   Psalm 22:7–18

Jesus knew exactly what was waiting for him in Jerusalem. Isn't it ironic that the only man in history who could truly escape death, who repeatedly demonstrated his mastery over it, deliberately *chose* to die? He could have walked through the crowd unscathed, as he had done many times before, but instead, Jesus chose death.

Then, in Matthew chapter 20, Jesus goes on to explain why all this must take place: he must give his life

"as a ransom for many."   Matthew 20:28

Today, we sometimes hear about a "ransom" being paid to release a hostage. In Jesus' day, it meant much the same: a "ransom" was often paid to release people from slavery.

But how is Jesus' death "a ransom"?

In the last two chapters, we caught a glimpse of how serious our sin really is. It is so serious, such a terrible offence against God himself, that it cannot simply be overlooked. It does matter. And there is a price to be paid for it, as Jesus' loving warnings about hell clearly show.

How can any of us pay that price? No amount of money, and no stockpile of "good deeds", can meet that ransom demand. It is impossible.

But there is a way – and only one way – that the ransom *can* be paid: the death of Jesus Christ, *as a ransom for many*.

It's the perfect plan because only a sinless person can pay the price for someone else's sin, and Jesus was sinless. Not even his enemies could find fault with him.

It's the perfect plan because it shows how loving God is. Jesus was prepared to die on behalf of even those who hate him. And although we are not the ones who actually put him up on the cross that Friday morning, all of us have silently wished that he would stay there. We have all wished that God would keep out of our business, our family life, our decision-making, our sexual relationships and our future plans. But despite this, as Romans chapter 5 verse 8 puts it, "God demonstrates his own love for us in this: While we were still sinners, Christ died for us."

It's the perfect plan because it shows how just God is. Jesus' death deals with sin in the right way. A perfect judge would never let the guilty go free, not without punishment. And that's why Jesus had to die "as a ransom for many". In Jesus, God was saying, "I must punish sin – otherwise, there's no justice. But I will serve the sentence myself, so that you don't have to." The perfect plan: justice is done, but at the same time, amazing love is demonstrated.

It's the perfect plan: God's justice demanded the ransom, God's love provided the ransom, and God himself *is* the ransom.

It was something Jesus was born to do. He did it willingly and lovingly. Even his name – which means "the Lord saves" – perfectly expresses the reason he died.

You're saying that Jesus *had* to die to save me?

There's one in every school. A kid who crept up behind you when you were about to cross a busy road, or when you were standing by the edge of the swimming pool, or if you were sitting near an open window, four storeys up.

Without warning he'd grab you and shout, "SAVED YOU!"

In that split second, you suddenly feel as if you're falling into the road, or into the swimming pool, or out of the window. And everybody finds it absolutely hilarious.

Except you. Because your heart has practically stopped with the shock of it. Because you're now red with embarrassment, having squealed like a startled pig. Because you were never in any real danger anyway. Do you remember who it was who used to do that in your school? I remember who it was in my school.

That's right. It was me. I'd scamper away, aching with laughter, but no-one else thought it was even slightly funny. Because – needless to say – I hadn't saved their lives at all. There was nothing for them to be saved from in the first place.

I think that's how some people feel when they're told about Jesus dying to save sinners. They feel like the Bible has crept up behind them, grabbed them by the shoulders and shouted, "Saved you!" And they respond, with some irritation, "I don't need saving! I'm not a sinner, and my so-called 'sins' are not a problem."

I don't say this lightly, but if that were true, Jesus would not have chosen to die as he did. How do we know this? Because in Matthew chapter 26 we are given a glimpse into the mind of Jesus, and it is tortured by the thought of going to the cross.

> Then Jesus went with his disciples to a place called Gethsemane, and he said to them, "Sit here while I go over there and pray." He took Peter and the two sons of Zebedee along with him, and he began to be sorrowful and troubled. Then he said to them, "My soul is overwhelmed with sorrow to the point of death. Stay here and keep watch with me."
>
> Going a little farther, he fell with his face to the ground and prayed, "My Father, if it is possible, may this cup be taken from me. Yet not as I will, but as you will."　　　Matthew 26:36–39

Jesus prayed that agonised prayer three times. The decision to die "as a ransom for many" was not taken easily. If even Jesus was "overwhelmed with sorrow" at the thought of bearing the punishment our sin deserves, our claims that sin doesn't really matter – or worse, that we don't need saving at all – seem naive at best. And if there were any other way of dealing with the problem of sin – a desperately serious problem, as the nature of Jesus' death graphically shows – then Jesus died for nothing.

At Arlington National Cemetery in Virginia, there is a gravestone with a simple inscription on it. It says this: "I want to stand where you're standing."[6] Underneath those words is the lovingly engraved story of an incident that occurred during the American Civil War. A Yankee soldier, only 19 years of age, was part of a firing squad, assigned to execute a man for treason. As he closed one eye and took aim down the barrel of his gun, he was horrified to see that he knew the man he was about to shoot. He lowered his gun, walked over to his captain, and said, "I can't do it. That man has a wife and children at home. If I shoot him, I not only end his life, but I end their lives too. I will make his wife a widow and I'll be robbing the children of their father. I can't do it."

So after a short discussion, they came up with a plan. They agreed that the young soldier could take the condemned man's place. The 19 year-old Yankee marched up to the Confederate captive and said simply, "I want to stand where you're standing."

The captive took off his blindfold and walked away. Back to his wife, his family, his life. But his freedom came at great cost to another: the young man who had willingly chosen to die in his place.

If the passers-by had got their way when they said, "Come down from the cross, if you are the Son of God!", we would all be lost. If he had come down, who else could've done what he did on our behalf? We would still be without hope in the world, alienated from our Creator,

---

[6] Quoted at http://www.christthetruth.org.uk/matt26.htm accessed 10th July 2007.

never to be forgiven. But because he is the Son of God –
perfectly just, perfectly loving – he chose not to come
down from the cross. And he did it willingly. As the
perfect, sinless substitute, he knew that he, and only he,
could stand in our place, and pay the price perfectly.

And if the religious leaders had got their way when
they said, "Let him come down from the cross, and we
will believe in him", then why believe in him at all? If he
had come down, there would be nothing and no-one to
believe in. There would be no ransom for sin, and no-one
willing to pay it,

"I want to stand where you're standing." The words
are a faint echo of the words spoken by Jesus two
thousand years earlier: "The Son of Man did not come to
be served, but to serve, and to give his life as a ransom for
many." He gave his life for yours because he loves you so
much. Not because you deserve his love; quite the
opposite. But that's how extraordinary, how relentless,
how selfless, how death-defying God's love is.

06

"If I Can Be Forgiven Everything, Doesn't That Mean I Can Do Whatever I Like?"

It was 8pm, and I'd just pressed the doorbell of a young couple who we'll call "Mr and Mrs Smith". They'd invited me round to hear more about why I'm a Christian. However, it turned out to be more than just the three of us.

"We've invited some of our friends here this evening to hear what you have to say," my hosts explained as they opened the door. I was handed a plate of food and walked into a room that was packed with expectant people.

"This is Paul, and as you know we've invited him over to tell us more about Christianity." Then Mr Smith looked at me and said, "Over to you."

I put down my plate and tried to explain, as clearly as I could, what I believed.

When I'd finished, someone in the room said, "Let me get this straight. Are you saying that no matter how bad a person has been, they can be forgiven by God and go to heaven?"

"Yes, that's exactly what I'm saying," I replied excitedly. "It's terrific news isn't it?"

"No!" came the indignant reply. "What about the murderer and the terrorist? Surely you're not telling us they can be forgiven too? No, I cannot accept that."

The shocking extent of God's generosity towards sinful human beings was demonstrated for us again and again by Jesus, and perhaps never more so than when he was hanging between two criminals, suffering the most painful death imaginable.

> One of the criminals who hung there hurled insults at him: "Aren't you the Christ? Save yourself and us!"
>
> But the other criminal rebuked him. "Don't you fear God," he said, "since you are under the same sentence? We are punished justly, for we are getting what our deeds deserve. But this man has done nothing wrong."
>
> Then he said, "Jesus, remember me when you come into your kingdom."
>
> Jesus answered him, "I tell you the truth, today you will be with me in paradise." Luke 23:39–43

A person executed on a cross was no petty criminal. Those condemned to such a dreadful punishment were typically rebellious slaves or enemies of the state. So dreadful was it that Roman citizens were usually exempt from the punishment, except in cases of high treason. In other words, it was reserved for the lowest of the low. The most disparaged and despised members of society. People that modern-day tabloids would describe as evil.

And what does it take for Jesus to forgive such a person? Nothing but an acknowledgement of guilt ("We are punished justly, for we are getting what our deeds deserve") and an expression of trust ("Jesus, remember me when you come into your kingdom.").

But how can God forgive evil so readily?
There is nothing cheap about the forgiveness God offers in Jesus Christ. He paid for it in suffering, bloodshed and

death. And God cannot be fooled. It's not as if God is hoodwinked if someone "pretends" to say sorry, just to get off the hook. As Psalm 44 says, God "knows the secrets of the heart."

The bottom line is this. If you sincerely long to be forgiven, it doesn't matter what you've done, or how late in life you put your trust in Jesus. His death on the cross is more than enough to earn you that forgiveness, and ensure that you spend eternity with him "in paradise".

In Matthew chapter 20, Jesus tells the story of a landowner who pays people to work in his vineyard. Some he employs early in the day, others he employs "at the eleventh hour". Then the time comes to pay the men their wages:

> "The workers who were hired about the eleventh hour came and each received a denarius. So when those came who were hired first, they expected to receive more. But each one of them also received a denarius. When they received it, they began to grumble against the landowner. 'These men who were hired last worked only one hour,' they said, 'and you have made them equal to us who have borne the burden of the work and the heat of the day.'
>
> "But he answered one of them, 'Friend, I am not being unfair to you. Didn't you agree to work for a denarius? Take your pay and go. I want to give the man who was hired last the same as I gave you. Don't I have the right to do what I want with my own money? Or are you envious because I am generous?'" Matthew 20:9–15

God's generosity is such that he gives freely to whoever he chooses. We may feel that we deserve God's forgiveness far more than other people. Some of the guests at my surprise party certainly did. But the fact is that *none* of us

<u>deserve *anything* from God.</u> We should be profoundly grateful for his generosity, not find ways to begrudge it.

But if God forgives so freely and generously, doesn't that mean I can live any way I want?

Let me tell you another "party" story. This one happened two thousand years ago, but you can still feel the embarrassment of the guests, even today. The details are recorded for us in Luke chapter 7 onwards:

> Now one of the Pharisees invited Jesus to have dinner with him, so he went to the Pharisee's house and reclined at the table.
> Luke 7:36

But this Pharisee – a religious leader called Simon – was about to get a thoroughly unwelcome guest:

> When a woman who had lived a sinful life in that town learned that Jesus was eating at the Pharisee's house, she brought an alabaster jar of perfume, and as she stood behind him at his feet weeping, she began to wet his feet with her tears. Then she wiped them with her hair, kissed them and poured perfume on them.
>
> When the Pharisee who had invited him saw this, he said to himself, "If this man were a prophet, he would know who is touching him and what kind of woman she is – that she is a sinner."
> Luke 7:37–39

But Jesus knew exactly what kind of a woman she was. She was a prostitute, dirty and reviled, and her dishevelled presence must have made the other party guests very uncomfortable.

Like any accomplished gatecrasher trying to gain entry to a party without invitation, she'd brought a bottle – in this case, an alabaster jar of perfume. But unlike your typical partygoer, she was weeping. She wept and wept, so that her tears of joy were enough to wash Jesus' feet. Overflowing with love for Jesus, her hair becomes a makeshift cloth to dry them with, the perfume, a lavish demonstration of her devotion to him. And as the heady scent reaches into every corner of the Pharisee's house, Jesus tells him a story that explains the woman's extraordinary behaviour. It also reveals why a person forgiven by God will never again "live any way they want."

> "Two men owed money to a certain money-lender. One owed him five hundred denarii, and the other fifty. Neither of them had the money to pay him back, so he cancelled the debts of both. Now which of them will love him more?"
>
> Simon replied, "I suppose the one who had the bigger debt cancelled."
>
> "You have judged correctly," Jesus said.   Luke 7:41–43

There is only one response you and I are capable of when we truly understand how much we have been forgiven: love.

The woman knew that the way she'd lived her life had put her greatly in God's debt, with no means to pay those debts off. But wonderfully, God had offered to cancel that debt. Having been rescued from such a desperate situation, the last thing the woman wanted to do was go back to her previous life. Instead, "she loved much":

> Then [Jesus] turned toward the woman and said to Simon, "Do you see this woman? I came into your house. You did not give me any water for my feet, but she wet my feet with her tears and wiped them with her hair. You did not give me a kiss, but this woman, from the time I entered, has not stopped kissing my feet. You did not put oil on my head, but she has

> poured perfume on my feet. Therefore, I tell you, her many sins have been forgiven – for she loved much. But he who has been forgiven little loves little."
>
> Luke 7:44–47

Ironically, those people – like Simon the Pharisee – who think of themselves as most respectable, most religious or most morally upright are often the very people who do not love God as they should. Why? *Because they do not see themselves as sinners to be forgiven. They see themselves as good people to be rewarded.* The result is a dutiful, self righteous, unloving life that says all the right things, is seen in all the right places, but experiences no real love for God. The woman, by contrast, knows very well that she is a sinner who has been freely forgiven by God's grace. And the result is a life poured out as lavishly and joyfully as perfume from an alabaster jar.

Because she knew how much she'd been forgiven, she loved Jesus. And that love was shown outwardly by her actions: the tears, the kisses, the perfume. Once she felt that terrible burden of guilt lifted from her shoulders, the inexpressible joy, there was never any question of going back to her former life. It would be absurd, like jumping back into a river you've just been rescued from.

If I can be forgiven everything, doesn't that mean I can do whatever I like? No-one who understands how much they've been forgiven would ever want to live like that. No-one who knows how sinful they are, what it cost Jesus to gain them forgiveness, and how wonderful it is to be freely forgiven, will then walk away and live life "their own way". Jesus puts it quite explicitly when he says, "If you love me, you will obey what I command."[1]

---

[1] John 14:15.

And it's important to realise that the woman served Jesus *because* she'd been forgiven, not in order *to be* forgiven. Religion is "I obey, therefore I'm accepted." Christianity is "I'm accepted, therefore I obey".[2] That's a truth the woman instinctively understood, and it moved her to tears.

The only question for us is this: do we identify with Simon the Pharisee, or do we identify with the woman? Do we begrudge God's generosity because it seems unnecessary to us, or do we rejoice in it because we see just how much of it we need?

---

[2] Tim Keller, http://www.redeemer2.com/resources/papers/centrality.pdf accessed 10th July 2007.

07

"How Can Anyone Be Sure There's Life After Death?"

In 1985, Joe Simpson and his friend Simon Yates decided to climb a 21,000 foot high mountain in Peru. About halfway through the ascent, Simpson fell and smashed the bones in his right leg. Yates tried to lower him down the mountain on a rope, but it soon became clear that Simpson's weight was pulling them both off the mountain. Eventually, Yates made the agonising decision to cut the rope and he watched as Simpson plummeted down into the darkness of a huge crevasse. Giving him up for dead, Yates returned to base camp.

However, Simpson survived the fall. And he spent the next three-and-a-half excruciating days inching tortuously down the mountain, with no food and no water.

Later, he wrote about what it was that drove him on, despite the unbearable pain that wracked him every time he made the tiniest movement: "What was terrible was knowing I was going to die alone. I've never got over it and I don't think I ever will. When I had accepted in my heart that I was going to die, why did I keep crawling over those rocks, causing myself so much pain? I'm sure it was because if I was going to die, I wanted someone to hold me. And for a rough, tough mountaineer, that was a pathetic thing to be left with, wasn't it?"[1]

---

[1] Joe Simpson, interviewed by Sue Summers in *The Daily Telegraph*, October 2003.

Not all of us have stared death in the face. But many of us have been as close as we want to be, standing at the funerals of friends, family members. And whenever I take a funeral, I begin with these words:

> "I am the resurrection and the life. He who believes in me will live, even though he dies; and whoever lives and believes in me will never die."
> John 11:25–26

Jesus himself was at the funeral of a friend when he said this. But far from being mournful, they are powerful words which hold out the certain hope of life after death. Jesus is claiming that if people believe in him, they will be resurrected from the dead and live forever. And as if to prove his claim beyond any doubt, Jesus himself did just that.

Sometimes, a few words are enough to change your whole world. For me, it was three little words, spoken on 13th June 1992. It was a warm summer evening in a beautiful English town called Windsor. I was sitting on a balcony in a restaurant overlooking the Thames, and I plucked up the courage to ask my companion a question that had been on my mind for some time: "Will you marry me?"

And then Caroline responded with three little words that had a profound effect on the subsequent course of my life: "Shut your face."

Actually, she didn't say that. But she could've done. What she actually said was, "Yes I will", but imagine how different my life would've been if the three words she spoke had been something else, if they'd been: "I feel sick" or "Get the bill" or "Ha ha ha". What a difference three words can make.

One other example I'd give would be the three words spoken towards the end of Matthew's Gospel. Just three words, but words with such far-reaching implications that no-one on earth is unaffected by them. Are you ready? Here they are: <u>"He has risen"</u>.

You're probably unimpressed after all that build-up, aren't you?

But the historical event that lies behind those three words changes our lives forever. Because those words "He has risen" were spoken – three days after Jesus' agonising and very public death on a cross in first-century Palestine – by someone Matthew describes as "an angel of the Lord", sitting outside an empty tomb which only hours before had held the dead body of Jesus Christ.[2]

Even assuming for a moment that Jesus _had_ been resurrected, what difference does it make to me?

I remember having a tuberculosis vaccination at school. In the few weeks leading up to the injection, all the older kids in the school took great pleasure in making up stories about what happened on the other side of the nurse's door: "I knew this one kid, right, and his whole arm went blue and fell off. He never played cricket again." You know the kind of thing.

Anyway, the fateful day arrived, and even though I suspected the stories might not be true, I was still scared. All the kids in our year were lined up outside the nurse's door in single file and – worse still – alphabetical order, so I was right at the end of the queue. I began to wonder if they used the same needle on everyone, and if so, how blunt it would be by the time they got to me. The long wait seemed to be dragging on and on, and as the minutes passed, so my fear grew and grew.

---

[2] Matthew 28:6.

I remember fixing my eyes on scrawny little Peter Hopkins, further up the line. I was grateful for Peter, not least because he deflected attention by being the only thirteen year-old less muscular than me. Peter Hopkins is so thin, went the joke, that when he has a shower in the morning, he has to run around to get wet.

I kept looking at him, thinking that if *he* could get in and out of that nurse's office alive and with both arms still attached to his body, then *I* could too.

And when I saw him do just that, it felt amazing.

Peter "When I go to the park, ducks throw *me* bread" Hopkins had gone through the nurse's door, and had returned to tell the tale. He even looked cheerful about it.

To read of Jesus' death and resurrection is to fix our eyes on the first and only person who has ever gone through death, and overcome it completely, never to die again. If we're following him, death no longer holds any fear because we've seen him go through it unscathed. In fact, it's even more than that: Jesus has demonstrated that he is death's *master*. To put our trust in him is to know that death will have no more hold on us than it had on him.

But how do I know he even died in the first place? Maybe he wasn't dead when they put him in the tomb, then he simply revived and escaped?

All the evidence suggests that Jesus was stone dead when he was placed in the tomb. John, an actual eyewitness of Jesus' death on the cross, tells us:

> Because the Jews did not want the bodies left on the crosses during the Sabbath, they asked Pilate to have the legs broken and the bodies taken down. The soldiers therefore came and

> broke the legs of the first man who had been crucified with
> Jesus, and then those of the other. But when they came to
> Jesus and found that he was already dead, they did not break
> his legs.   John 19:31–33

Roman soldiers, especially those in charge of executions, were expert killers. They broke the legs of those hanging on crosses in order to bring about death quickly (basically, you could no longer use your legs to support your breathing, so you suffocated in a matter of minutes). This they did to the two criminals hanging either side of Jesus. After all, having been commanded by the Roman Governor, Pontius Pilate, to make absolutely sure that the sentence of execution was fully carried out, they didn't want to take any chances. To fail in their duty would mean that they would face execution themselves. That being the case, and considering that they did not break Jesus' legs, the soldiers must have been completely satisfied that Jesus was dead.

Nevertheless, we then read that "one of the soldiers pierced Jesus' side with a spear, bringing a sudden flow of blood and water." Whatever the reason for this spear-thrust, it seems very unlikely that after all the beatings, the torture, the hours spent slowly bleeding on the cross, the spear-thrust, and the expert supervision of the soldiers, Jesus was simply unconscious.

Even if you *do* insist that Jesus was merely "out for the count", and that he woke up in the tomb, how can we explain his escape? His body was wrapped tightly in linen cloth, and covered in about seventy-five pounds of pungent anointing oil[3] – enough to suffocate a healthy

---

[3] "Nicodemus brought a mixture of myrrh and aloes, about seventy-five pounds. Taking Jesus' body, the two of them wrapped it, with the spices, in strips of linen. This was in accordance with Jewish burial customs." (John 19:39–40)

man, let alone someone who has just been crucified. The rock used to close the tomb was huge – around one and a half tons at a conservative estimate – and was rolled into a "groove" in front of the entrance. It needed many physically strong men to budge it. Again, is this a likely escape route for someone recently taken down from a Roman cross?

The body could've been stolen by his disciples, though, couldn't it?

Matthew chapter 27 gives us an interesting insight into that theory:

> …[T]he chief priests and the Pharisees went to Pilate. "Sir," they said, "we remember that while he was still alive that deceiver said, 'After three days I will rise again.' So give the order for the tomb to be made secure until the third day. Otherwise, his disciples may come and steal the body and tell the people that he has been raised from the dead. This last deception will be worse than the first."
>
> "Take a guard," Pilate answered. "Go, make the tomb as secure as you know how." So they went and made the tomb secure by putting a seal on the stone and posting the guard.
>
> Matthew 27:62–66

The Jewish and Roman authorities anticipate the possibility that the disciples could turn grave robbers, so they make absolutely sure that any attempt to steal the body will be impossible. It's worth noting that the "guard" mentioned could consist of anything between four and sixteen men, each knowing full well that if they failed in their duties, they would be executed.

Ironically, when the body *does* disappear, we read:

> …[S]ome of the guards went into the city and reported to the chief priests everything that had happened. When the chief priests had met with the elders and devised a plan, they gave the soldiers a large sum of money, telling them, "You are to say, 'His disciples came during the night and stole him away while we were asleep.' If this report gets to the governor, we will satisfy him and keep you out of trouble." So the soldiers took the money and did as they were instructed.   Matthew 28:11–15

So neither the Jewish authorities nor the tomb guards believe that Jesus' body was stolen by the disciples. It's the best story they can come up with to try and explain what actually happened. But they know that their story is a lie.

The truth is this. If anyone, at any time, had been able to produce Jesus' corpse, the whole Christian movement would have been utterly destroyed. I would not be writing this book, and you certainly wouldn't be reading it.

But no-one was able to produce Jesus' corpse, and expose the resurrection as a fraud. On the contrary, the Christian movement grew and grew, its leaders insisting that Jesus Christ had indeed died, but was resurrected three days later, just as he had promised.[4]

Of course the leaders insisted he was alive – they just wanted to attract more followers, didn't they?

It wasn't just the leaders who insisted he was alive. For example, in one book of the Bible, we read that five hundred people saw him at once,[5] a fact which also puts paid to idea that Jesus' resurrection was some kind of hallucination brought about by the wishful thinking of certain disciples.

---

[4] Jesus predicts his own death and resurrection repeatedly. For example, he says this in Mark 9:31: "The Son of Man is going to be betrayed into the hands of men. They will kill him, and after three days he will rise."
[5] 1 Corinthians 15:6.

And don't forget what the leaders had to lose by insisting he was alive. It was precisely because of this claim that they brought upon themselves opposition, persecution and even execution. Why give up your life for something you know is not true? After all, what's the point of having hundreds of followers if you're not alive to enjoy it?

They gave up their lives willingly because they were convinced of Jesus' resurrection, and therefore convinced there was life after death. They remembered Jesus' words: "I am the resurrection and the life. He who believes in me will live, even though he dies; and whoever lives and believes in me will never die."

And it's the same for Christians today. As they consider death, they too remember Jesus' words. They know that because he overcame death, they will overcome it. It's like a needle and thread. Wherever the needle has gone, the thread inevitably follows. When I'm connected to Christ I can be sure that because he went through death and came out the other side, I will too.

But what exactly will life after death be like? Won't it be a bit dull to spend an eternity in heaven sitting on clouds, playing harps?
I couldn't agree more, and I wouldn't want to go there if that was all it was.

But Jesus describes eternity as a place of security and endless unspoiled beauty, a place where "moth and rust do not destroy, and where thieves do not break in and steal."[6] He describes it as a "feast",[7] a place so glorious that all our wealth and worldly possessions immediately lose their appeal by comparison.[8] The last book of the Bible, Revelation, describes a place that is flawless and

---

[6] Matthew 6:20. [7] Matthew 8:11. [8] Matthew 13:44–46.

faultlessly suited to its inhabitants, where there will be "no more death or mourning or crying or pain."[9]

And the eternal destiny of Christians, as described in the Bible, is a physical place populated by people with physical bodies. It's not an abstract place, full of disembodied spirits who float around, well, playing harps on clouds. One of the extraordinary things about Jesus' resurrection body was that it could be touched and interacted with. It was *real*. After his resurrection, Jesus' followers met him, talked to him, and ate with him.[10]

Even Thomas, the most sceptical person of all. He hadn't been in the room when Jesus had shown himself to the other disciples, so when they said, "We have seen the Lord!", Thomas was having none of it. He insisted, "Unless I see the nail marks in his hands and put my finger where the nails were, and put my hand into his side, I will not believe." A week later the disciples were together again, and this time Thomas was with them. Though the doors were locked, Jesus came and stood among them and said, "Peace be with you!" Then he said to Thomas, "Put your finger here; see my hands. Reach out your hand and put it into my side." There's nothing abstract or dull about a man who is suddenly able to appear in a locked house, then invites people to reach out and touch the wounds that had brought about his death a few days earlier.

"Blessed are the meek", says Jesus in Matthew chapter 5 verse 5, "for they will inherit the earth." Once again, Jesus emphasises the fact that eternity will be a tangible place. But we won't be inheriting the earth in its current form. Instead, when God brings history to a close, he will create "a new heaven and a new earth",[11] a place untouched by human sin, and exquisite in its perfection.

---

[9] Revelation 21:4. [10] These events are recorded in John 20 and 21. [11] Revelation 21:1.

In an interview, the writer V.S. Naipaul said, "From time to time – and this is probably true of all people – there is a sentence that comes into my head, and the sentence is, 'It's time for me to go back home now.' For me, it does not mean anything. But it is there all the same."[12] Like most of us, he already has an inkling of what eternity will really be like, the place Jesus describes as "my Father's house".[13]

And how do we get to the Father's house? Just days before his execution, Jesus took his disciples aside to teach them, amongst other things, what his death would achieve. The disciples were understandably distressed as he spoke of his "going away". Seeing their concern, he spoke these magnificent words to them:

> "Do not let your hearts be troubled. Trust in God; trust also in me. In my Father's house are many rooms; if it were not so, I would have told you. I am going there to prepare a place for you. And if I go and prepare a place for you, I will come back and take you to be with me that you also may be where I am."   John 14:1–3

How does Jesus "prepare a place" for his followers? By dying on the cross for them.

Having been left behind by his climbing companion Simon Yates, the question that mountaineer Joe Simpson gets asked all the time is this: "Would you have done the same thing in Simon's position?" His answer is always the same. "Simon put his life at risk to save mine, and then got in a situation where he knew he was likely to die. No-one you know – or will ever know – will die for someone else in those circumstances."[14]

Thankfully, Joe Simpson is wrong about that.

---

[12] V.S. Naipaul, interviewed by Tim Adams in *The Observer*, September 2004. [13] John 14:2.
[14] Joe Simpson, interviewed by Jasper Reeves in *The Week*, 15 November 2003.

08

"What About Followers Of Other Religions?"

Raël wasn't always a messenger from outer space. He used to be a French motoring journalist called Claude.

However, in 1973, at the age of 26, everything changed for Claude. He got up as usual, jumped in his car, and headed off to work, but then carried on driving "as if I was being guided." He continued driving until he reached an extinct volcano in the Auvergne region of France. There he found a silver spaceship, out of which stepped a small bearded person. "His skin was white with a lightly greenish tinge, a bit like someone with liver trouble." The bearded creature announced that the elders of the Planet Elohim had chosen Claude to spread their message: that God and evolution are myths, and that the Elohim had created life on earth.

Spreading the word hasn't always been easy, Raël says. "At first, it was a nightmare. People, they laughed at me. Oh yes. They thought I was crazy." But he persevered, and now finds himself surrounded by people who call him "Your Holiness", their reverential gaze falling upon a man wearing a white satin suit, quilted shoulder pads and a cripplingly large medallion. His thinning hair is pulled into a topknot.

Raël pours scorn on other people who claim to have met aliens. "They have problems," he says. "There is only one messenger."[1]

Well, who's to say that Raël is wrong? Perhaps the most unnerving thing about Raël – and there are many – is his apparently unshakeable sincerity. He clearly believes the things he says, and so do his followers.

Exactly. Surely the main thing is that you're sincere in your belief? *You can be sincere, but wrong*

Is sincerity all God cares about? Let's look at an encounter between Jesus and a devout, sincere Jew called Nicodemus. The meeting is recorded for us in John chapter 3, where we see that Nicodemus is not only sincere in his faith, he is a formidable theologian – probably the best of his day. In verse 10 Jesus describes him as "Israel's teacher" or more literally "*the* teacher of Israel." He's the kind of speaker people would've travelled miles to hear. And what was the first thing Jesus said to him? "I tell you the truth, no-one can see the Kingdom of God unless he is *born again*."[2]

Before we consider exactly what those two words mean, it's worth noticing what Jesus *doesn't* say. Jesus doesn't say, "I tell you the truth, no-one can see the Kingdom of God unless he is sincere in his own beliefs." And yet a lot of people believe just that: it doesn't matter particularly what you believe, as long as you believe it sincerely. It sounds plausible at first, but, as author Michael Green points out:

> You never hear it when people are talking about the horrors of Auschwitz or Belsen. Hitler was undoubtedly sincere in his

---

[1] Interviewed by John Preston in *The Sunday Telegraph*, April 2003. [2] John 3:3, my italics.

> hatred of the Jewish people, but everyone would admit he
> was wrong... An example like this, which caused the
> annihilation of millions of people, should make us very
> cautious about claiming that it does not matter what you
> believe as long as you are sincere... [S]incerity is not enough.
> I may sincerely believe that all airplanes at London Airport will
> take me to America, but I would be wrong. I may sincerely
> believe that lots of cream and chocolate is the best way to
> recuperate after a heart attack, but I would be wrong.[3]

"As long as you're sincere". We don't think that way about anything else. The man who killed 32 people before killing himself on the campus at Virginia Tech was undoubtedly sincere – I cannot imagine anyone killing themselves *insincerely* – but few of us point to his sincerity as evidence that he was right to do what he did.

But surely God will accept moral, religious people?

Back to Nicodemus. He was a Pharisee and a member of the Jewish ruling council. He would have been a regular at the synagogue, he would have made sacrifices in the temple, he would have prayed often and given generously. What's more, as a member of the Jewish Ruling Council, Nicodemus needed to be a well-respected, morally upright citizen. If anyone was going to be accepted by God on religious or moral grounds, it was Nicodemus.

But remember what Jesus says to him: "I tell you the truth, *no-one* can see the Kingdom of God *unless he is born again.*" If we're tempted to trust in our own religious practices to get us into heaven, Jesus' statement here should stop us in our tracks. There's only one way you'll enter God's Kingdom, says Jesus, and it's by being "born again."

---

[3] Michael Green, *But Don't All Religions Lead to God?* (Sovereign World, 2002).

Whatever Jesus means by this phrase, it is pretty clear what it does *not* mean. It certainly doesn't mean that a person must literally "enter a second time into his mother's womb to be born", as Nicodemus realises.[4] What it *does* mean, however, is no less startling. Jesus explains that to be "born again" means to receive from God nothing less than a completely new life: a completely transformed, completely forgiven life. Amazingly, Jesus is telling even a man like Nicodemus, with his impressive moral and religious credentials, that in order for him to be accepted by God, God must completely remake him. From scratch.

The reason we (and Nicodemus) need to be "born again" in this way is because nothing less than a completely new beginning can put right all that is wrong with us. Why? Because according to Jesus, we're a write-off – spiritually speaking. Nothing is salvageable. "This is the verdict", Jesus tells Nicodemus, "Light has come into the world, *but men loved darkness instead of light because their deeds were evil*."[5] According to Jesus, we always choose darkness over light. And we don't simply choose darkness, we *love* darkness.

A friend of mine told me about a woman he knew who was having an affair. She said that whenever her lover came to her house, she deliberately picked up all the framed photographs of her husband, and turned them face down. While having sex with the other man, she did not want to make eye contact with her husband – even if it was only a picture of his eyes.

Many of us feel a similar sense of shame and discomfort when we make eye contact with God. That's

---

[4] John 3:4. [5] John 3:19, my italics.

why we love darkness instead of light: we think the darkness enables us to do whatever we want, without ever having to give an account of our actions to anyone else. We prefer to turn all reminders of God "face down", so that we never have to make eye contact with him.

And in God's eyes, even the moral, religious deeds of Nicodemus are "evil" because those deeds flow from a darkness-loving heart which is evil through and through. Our hearts are like a polluted spring of water. Because the spring itself is polluted, every last drop of water that flows from that spring is tainted. Jesus' implication is unnerving and clear: unless we're to be lost forever, we need to be forgiven, and we need a completely new, radically different heart: one that loves God. One that loves the light instead of the darkness.

So how do we get this new beginning? Being sincere is not enough. Being moral or religious is not enough, as Nicodemus discovered. And, as most of us have discovered if we've ever tried to turn over a new leaf, sheer will power is not enough. If we can't cause our rebirth any more than we caused ourselves to be born in the first place, if we can't make ourselves be "born again" any more than a dead person can make themselves come back to life, then quite frankly, what are we supposed to do? *Jesus is asking the impossible.*

Yes, he is.

He does it so that we will run to the only one for whom *all* things are possible: the only one who has the power to raise the dead and create new life with a word. Jesus expects Nicodemus to know who he is talking about. He says to him, "You are Israel's teacher and do you not understand these things?"[6] Jesus expects this

---

[6] John 3:10.

teacher to remember the things he's been teaching, like this passage from the book of Ezekiel, where God says:

> "I will give you a new heart and put a new spirit[7] in you; I will remove from you your heart of stone and give you a heart of flesh."
>
> Ezekiel 36:26, my italics

He expects him to know that <u>only God can give us this new heart.</u> Only he can enable us to be reborn. At the beginning of John's Gospel, it's put like this:

> Yet to all who received [Jesus], to those who believed in his name, he gave the right to become children of God – children born not of natural descent, nor of human decision or a husband's will, but born of God.
>
> John 1:12–13

No other religion or moral regime or person or programme can give us the new birth that Jesus says we so desperately need.

And *nothing else* can deal with our sin. When Jesus is talking to Nicodemus about being "born again", he also describes it as being born "of water".[8] And once again, Nicodemus should have understood the implication. Once again, Ezekiel should have been ringing in his ears:

> [God says:] "I will sprinkle clean water on you, and you will be clean; I will cleanse you from all your impurities…"
>
> Ezekiel 36:25

The promise here is that we will be forgiven and cleansed from *all our sins*. As we've seen in previous chapters, sin is so serious that it takes something – and someone – unique to deal with it. Nothing else will do.

---

[7] This is God's Spirit, promised by Jesus to all those who love him (John 14:15–17). [8] John 3:5.

If there *were* any other way of overcoming the separation between us and God, any other way that we could have the joy of knowing God, would God have given his only Son to die?

So what about other religions?

Many religions agree that human beings are disconnected from the divine in some way. But the answers they give to this problem are not the same. In fact, they completely contradict each other. That means that although these answers could all be wrong, they cannot all be right. If I say that penguins live exclusively north of the equator, and you say that they live exclusively south of the equator, we could both be wrong. Or one of us could be right. But there's no way we can *both* be right.

So the question that remains is this: are *any* of these answers right? Do *any* of them offer a satisfying solution to the sin that separates us from God?

Into this confusion, Jesus speaks clearly and compassionately: "*I* am the way and the truth and the life. No-one comes to the Father *except through me.*"[9]

All of us sincerely believe something. The only question is: are we sincerely believing the truth, or something else?

According to current estimates, Raël has around 60,000 followers.

---

[9] John 14:6, my italics.

09

"Isn't Faith Just A Psychological Crutch?"

"So why are you flying to Belfast? You live there?" He was an American undergraduate, off to visit a friend from back home.

"No, I'm giving a few talks from the Bible at an event North of Belfast."

This is usually the point at which I'm left to finish my newspaper. But he continued.

"Have you always been religious? How did you come to work in the church?"

A few minutes later, after the steward had given us each a cup of orange juice and a plastic pack of pretzels, the undergraduate said something I've heard many times before and since: "I wish I had your faith."

"But you can," I insisted.

I could tell he wasn't convinced. As we talked on, it became clear that – to him – faith was something he could simply never have. It required some almighty inner mustering, or a natural propensity to believe unquestioningly, perhaps. Some fateful chromosome allowed me to "have faith", while he was somehow destined to live life without it.

He was right though, wasn't he? Some people can just accept religious things, while others are more sceptical aren't they?

To be fair, I don't entirely blame people for taking that view. There are some Christians who seem decidedly confused about what faith is. I've heard one or two answer questions about God by saying, "Ah well, that's where you've just got to have faith!" Pardon me for saying so, but the person who says that probably doesn't know the answer to the question and is almost certainly too lazy to find out. It's that kind of answer that has led many to believe that faith is the unthinking acceptance of things we can't possibly understand. In other words, good old "blind" faith.

So what is faith, then, if it isn't that?

Towards the end of his Gospel, John writes, "Jesus did many other miraculous signs in the presence of his disciples, which are not recorded in this book. But these are written *that you may believe that Jesus is the Christ, the Son of God, and that by believing you may have life in his name.*"[1] The word "believe" here could just as accurately be translated "have faith" or even better "trust." So John's definition of faith is: *trusting in Jesus Christ because of the historical facts.*

And that's why I told the undergraduate he *could* have faith. The Bible never asks us to have faith in someone we can know nothing about. Quite the opposite, in fact; it encourages us to trust in someone we *can* know about. The only way we can determine whether or not there is any truth in Christianity – and whether it makes any sense to have faith – is by examining Jesus' life and teaching.

[1] John 20: 30–31, my italics.

Why would you need to believe in Jesus unless your own life is lacking somehow?

It's true that Jesus welcomes those who feel their lives are lacking somehow:

> "Come to me, all you who are weary and burdened, and I will give you rest. Take my yoke upon you and learn from me, for I am gentle and humble in heart, and you will find rest for your souls." Matthew 11: 28–29

But actually, if you don't feel like that, and you're convinced that there really is nothing lacking in your life, then, to quote my travelling companion, "I wish I had your faith."

Jesus always taught that those who were convinced of their own spiritual health would not be interested in him. "It is not the healthy who need a doctor," he says in Matthew 9 verse 12. But, as we saw in the last chapter, Jesus' honest diagnosis of all humankind is that *no-one* is spiritually healthy. If we look at our own lives and the state of the world we live in, and conclude that all is well, says Jesus, then quite frankly, we're in denial.

I'll never forget the time I went to visit an elderly member of the church I was working at. He had been too ill to come to church for a couple of weeks and I'd already been told that he was really quite unwell. Nevertheless, when I went to see him, I was shocked at how quickly he had deteriorated. Later, as I said goodbye and made my way to the door, his wife stopped me and said: "Don't tell him, but he's got cancer."

It seemed amazing to me that no-one was telling him the truth about his own health. He must've known something was wrong, but no-one – not his wife, nor his doctor, nor any of his friends or family – wanted him to know how serious things had got. It was a conspiracy of silence, intended to try and keep his spirits up, but allowing the man no time to sort out his affairs, say his goodbyes and make his peace with God.

How many of us inch silently toward death without ever facing the fact that we are slowly dying? And if we won't admit that we're spiritually sick, then Jesus' offer of life and spiritual health is not for us: "It is not the healthy who need a doctor," said Jesus, "but the sick... I have not come to call the righteous, but sinners."

So, yes, absolutely: Christianity is for the weak, the spiritually sick. And according to Jesus, that's all of us – whether or not we realise it yet.

So it is for the weak, then?

In one way, yes.

But in another, definitely not. Having faith in Jesus is not for the faint of heart. Jesus says this in Luke chapter 9:

> "If anyone would come after me, he must deny himself and take up his cross daily and follow me. Whoever wants to save his life will lose it, but whoever loses his life for me will save it."
>
> Luke 9:23–24

Take a moment to consider what those words would mean for you and your life. Bear in mind that when those words were first spoken, the phrase "take up your cross" would have brought terrifying images to mind, images of shame, torture, punishment and death. That's what happened when a convicted criminal "took up their cross" and staggered under the weight of it to their place of crucifixion.

And Jesus says that his followers must take up their cross *daily.* If only every person who claims to be a

Christian lived like this: dying to self, being prepared to suffer daily, giving up their lives for the sake of others and for Christ. I say this knowing that there are many who call themselves Christian and who do *not* live like this. History speaks darkly of those who have not obeyed these words, and have even killed in the name of Christ. But read them again. *Jesus tells us to die for him, not kill for him.* He tells us to give our lives to others, not take the lives of others. True followers of Christ seek to alleviate or endure suffering, they don't seek to cause it.

Listen, for example, to this first-hand description of what happened to one of Jesus' first-century followers:

> Five times I have received…forty lashes minus one. Three times I was beaten with rods, once I was stoned, three times I was shipwrecked, I spent a night and a day in the open sea, I have been constantly on the move. I have been in danger from rivers, in danger from bandits, in danger from my own countrymen, in danger from Gentiles; in danger in the city, in danger in the country, in danger at sea; and in danger from false brothers. I have laboured and toiled and often gone without sleep; I have known hunger and thirst and have often gone without food; I have been cold and naked.

2 Corinthians 11:24–27

Nothing changes. Today, followers of Christ are hounded out of their homes, separated from their families, imprisoned, beaten, tortured and murdered for the sake of their faith. As I write, it's happening in the Sudan, Myanmar, Indonesia, Pakistan, Nigeria, China and many other countries around the world.

And all this is to say nothing of the Christian whose faith invites a subtler sort of suffering. Like a friend of mine whose father said to him, simply and sadly, "Aren't you taking all this too seriously?" Or the colleague whose best friends at university told him, "We just can't respect you intellectually any more." Or the person passed over for promotion, quietly overlooked when the party invitations get sent, and politely ignored in the office cafeteria. Death by a thousand papercuts is death nevertheless.

Christian faith is not a self-help philosophy, and it's not a psychological crutch. How many successful self-help philosophies are liable to cause unnatural and premature death? What kind of psychological crutch rewards the user with suffering and persecution?

It was faith, after all, that led to the imprisonment of Paul, one of the most celebrated figures in Christian history. Ironically, this was the man who only a few years before was himself throwing Christians into prison – even murdering Christians – so intense was his hatred for them. But now, having encountered Jesus for himself, he is unable to deny what he knows is true. And he begins to experience for himself the physical hardship of following Christ.

He is being held in prison in Caesarea, when King Agrippa asks to see Paul for himself. Brought before the king and some other officials, Paul explains how and why he became a Christian. He tells him the gospel, how Jesus was sent by God to suffer, die and rise from death in order to pay the price for human sin. He tells the king that the proper response to this is to "repent and turn to God", and to demonstrate that repentance by living a changed life.

At this point, Festus, the local governor, interrupts:

> "You are out of your mind, Paul!" he shouted. "Your great learning is driving you insane." Acts 26:24

This is not the first time a Christian has been accused of talking nonsense. However, Paul answers him calmly.

> "I am not insane, most excellent Festus," Paul replied. "What I am saying is true and reasonable." Acts 26:25

Faith in Jesus Christ is "reasonable". There is no such thing as blind, unthinking faith where Paul is concerned. He continues:

> "The king is familiar with these things, and I can speak freely to him. I am convinced that none of this has escaped his notice, because it was not done in a corner." Acts 26:26

Paul insists that the reasons for his own faith are there for all to see. The suffering, death and resurrection of Jesus were not events that occurred "in a corner". They happened openly, publicly. There was no-one living in Jerusalem who could claim to be ignorant of the facts.

> Then Agrippa said to Paul, "Do you think that in such a short time you can persuade me to be a Christian?"
>
> Paul replied, "Short time or long – I pray God that not only you but all who are listening to me today may become what I am, except for these chains." Acts 26:28–29

We're living at a distance of two thousand years now, but the events of Jesus' life have not changed. They have been recorded, as John's Gospel openly tells us, so that we "may believe that Jesus is the Christ, the Son of God, and that by believing you may have life in his name." These things have been written down in the Bible so that, as Luke puts it, "you may know the certainty of the things you have been taught."[2]

Investigate the certainty of these things. Faith shouldn't be blind at all. The author Carl Sagan,

---

[2] Luke 1:4.

an atheist, wrote, "It is better to grasp the universe as it really is than to persist in delusion, however satisfying and reassuring."[3]

I couldn't agree more.

---

[3] Carl Sagan, *The Demon-Haunted World* (Ballantyne Books, 1997).

10

"Why Do You Allow Suffering?"

The tower took years to build, and seconds to fall. It had stood as a powerful symbol of strength, security and prosperity, but it had given out its final breath, sending plumes of dust deep into the surrounding streets. With the building levelled to the ground, the death toll reverberating around the shaken city, and the rescue services long since departed, the skyline looked mournfully for something no longer there.

When Jesus talked about this tragedy – the collapse of the tower at Siloam, killing eighteen people – he knew it would not be the last. "But unless you repent," he said to those trying to make sense of the calamity, "you too will all perish."[1]

Recently, I got drawn into a drama about a New York firefighter troubled by his memories of those he has been unable to save. In one scene, he talks to a psychotherapist about his experiences:

> Three years ago, there was a fire six storeys up – one bedroom apartment, fifteen people living in it – and I find a little girl. Hurt pretty bad, holding a kitten. So I bring her down, six storeys, She's crying at me the whole time, saying, "Please Mr Fireman, please save my kitten, please don't let anything happen to my kitten, Mr Fireman."

---
[1] Luke 13:5.

Anyway, long story short. Cat lived. She didn't.

9/11, we lost four guys from this fire department, one of them was my cousin Jimmy…

He stops talking for a few seconds, unable to speak.

My best friend. Best fireman I ever worked with. Good family man, dedicated American… and every day I gotta drive to work, I drive through my neighbourhood, I see guys – drunken fools that I went to High School with – they're standing on the corner, high, having a great time, and I gotta wonder why these idiots are still walking around when Jimmy Keefe ain't.

Another long pause.

My cousin the priest says it's because it's all part of God's plan, like God's got a plan. You know what? If there is a God, he's got a whole lot of explaining to do.

The need for an explanation echoes throughout the Bible, too:

O LORD… I would speak with you about your justice:
Why does the way of the wicked prosper?   Jeremiah 12:1

How long, O LORD, must I call for help,
    but you do not listen?
Or cry out to you, "Violence!"
    but you do not save?
Why do you make me look at injustice?
    Why do you tolerate wrong?
Destruction and violence are before me;
    there is strife, and conflict abounds.   Habakkuk 1:2–3

My soul is in anguish.
    How long, O LORD, how long?   Psalm 6:3

Or, as the firefighter bluntly puts it, "He's got a whole lot of explaining to do."

Whether it is the face of a starving child on the news or the face of a loved one in a cancer hospice, when we meet suffering ourselves, the thought sometimes whispers to us: *there is no God ruling the universe at all.*

That's right, though, isn't it? Isn't it more realistic in the face of suffering just to accept that there is no God?
This scenario – a world without God – is also imagined by the writer of a book called Ecclesiastes in the Bible, and it leads him to three devastating conclusions.

Firstly, without God, there is no justice:

> I saw something else under the sun: In the place of judgement
> – wickedness was there, in the place of justice – wickedness
> was there.   Ecclesiastes 3:16

Not long after school began on Wednesday, March 13th, 1996, forty-three year-old Thomas Hamilton walked into the playground of a primary school in Dunblane, Scotland, carrying four guns. He made his way to the gym where Gwen Mayor was teaching a class of five and six year-olds and within three minutes, sixteen children and their teacher were dead. The massacre only ended when the man turned the gun on himself. Of twenty-nine children in the class, only one escaped physically unscathed.

The day after the tragedy occurred, a television debate tried to come to terms with what had happened. One of the guests said this: "The worst thing for the parents is the thought that justice will never be done." In other words, because Thomas Hamilton had taken his own life, he would never be held accountable for killing their children.

That is absolutely and unavoidably true – if there is no God. If there is no perfectly just God who will one day call every man and woman to account for their actions, then justice will never be done.

But thankfully, as Jesus makes clear by his words and by his very existence, we do not live in a godless universe. Thankfully, as Ecclesiastes goes on to assure us, "God will bring to judgement both the righteous and the wicked." In fact, the date is already circled on the calendar, and the name of the judge has already been announced:

> "For [God] has set a day when he will judge the world with justice by the man he has appointed. He has given proof of this to all men by raising him from the dead." Acts 17:31

The Bible describes it as "that great and dreadful day of the LORD"[2]: "dreadful" for those who have rejected the judge, Jesus Christ; "great" because it will finally bring all injustice to account. So firstly, without God there can be no justice, and no righting of wrongs.

Secondly, without God there is no future.

> All go to the same place; all come from dust, and to dust all return. Ecclesiastes 3:20

If there is no God, then death is the end, and that's that. This life is all we have, and nothing more. Janet Aitken, mother of an eleven year-old pupil at Dunblane primary school, said this in the aftermath of the tragedy: "I have my son, but many don't. When I saw my boy, I just wanted to weep, but many parents aren't having a reunion with their children." She's absolutely right. And, tragically, they never will – if there is no God.

But the Bible speaks clearly of a God who removes the sting of death. As Jesus says:

---

[2] Malachi 4:5.

> "I am the resurrection and the life. He who believes in me will live, even though he dies; and whoever lives and believes in me will never die."
> John 11:25–26

Without God, however, death is the end of all hope. Without God, there is no future.

Thirdly, and perhaps most devastating of all, without God there is no significance to human life.

> As for men [who say there is no God], God tests them so that they may see that they are like the animals.
> Ecclesiastes 3:18

If there is no God, then you and I are little more than animals with clothes on. This will be horrific, but let me take that thought to its logical conclusion. *When those children were slaughtered in that school, it was no more tragic an occurrence than a lion killing a gazelle on the plains of the Serengeti* – if there is no God.

When we watch the National Geographic channel and see one animal killing another, even another of the same species, how many of us stand up and indignantly object to the animal's cruelty? It's just "what animals do" as creatures of instinct. If we really are "like the animals", then the bloody events of Dunblane, Manhattan, Bali, Auschwitz, Cambodia, Virginia, and a thousand other places are no cause for pity, horror or anger. If there is no God, we should simply celebrate the fact that the fittest have survived.

But mercifully, as Jesus makes clear, human life is worth much more than that. God has made things that way: "Are not five sparrows sold for two pennies? Yet not one of them is forgotten by God. Indeed, the very hairs of your head are all numbered. Don't be afraid; you are worth more than many sparrows... how much more valuable you are than birds!"[3] Those who die are not forgotten, at least not by God.

The conclusion is this: if we decide to reject God out of hand because of the suffering we see in the world, then we must come to terms with something far worse than suffering: meaningless suffering. Because without God, there is no justice, no future and no significance to human life. The very thought fills the writer of Ecclesiastes with horror: "Meaningless! Meaningless! Utterly meaningless! Everything is meaningless."[4]

But if God exists, and suffering exists, what exactly is he going to do about it?

Jesus likened the situation to a field full of wheat – and weeds. The servants come and ask the field's owner if he wants them to pull the weeds up. Seems reasonable enough. Why not intervene and put an immediate end to these death-bringing parasites?

> "No," he answered, "because while you are pulling the weeds, you may root up the wheat with them. Let both grow together until the harvest. At that time I will tell the harvesters: First collect the weeds and tie them in bundles to be burned; then gather the wheat and bring it into my barn."
>
> Matthew 13:29–30

That, says Jesus, is the way of the world: good and bad existing together, inseparably linked – until the day the owner decides it's time for the harvest. At that point, what is good will be brought into the owner's glorious presence, and what is bad will be rejected.

That's why the Bible pleads with us, "Seek the LORD while he may be found; call on him while he is near."[5]

---

[3] Luke 12:6–7, 24. [4] Ecclesiastes 1:2. [5] Isaiah 55:6.

The truth is, we will not have this opportunity indefinitely. Considering how much evil there is in the world, considering the wilful disobedience and contempt that we continue to show our Creator day after day, year after year, God's "delay" in judging men and women – and bringing all suffering to an end – is evidence of his extraordinary patience and love. We should make good use of this borrowed time that God lends us.

A few years ago, even though I'd been living there for many years, I discovered a London I never knew existed. As I walked to work, there was a stillness I didn't recognise on the streets of London's West End. I looked around me: there were fewer cars on the road, fewer people walking the streets, and – yes, I wasn't imagining it – nothing in the sky. Unusually for human beings in London, one or two of us found ourselves making eye contact with other commuters, like paratroopers waiting to jump from a flak-battered plane. And this isn't some fitful dream I once had; it actually happened on Wednesday, September 12th, 2001.

At our service that lunchtime, we welcomed people who'd not been to church for years, and some who had never been. There was fear and anger and vulnerability on people's faces. Some clearly suspected that the attacks in New York and Washington were only the beginning, like the newspaper reporter who had written that very morning, "If New York is not safe, if the Pentagon is not safe, then quite simply, it is not safe." Some of them came asking God to protect them and their family, others came to pray for colleagues and friends who might have been caught up in the devastation, others came asking questions born of insecurity, confusion and indignation.

And most of the questions were neither aggressive nor accusing. They were carefully reasoned and genuinely offered. They were the very questions which had been left unasked and unanswered as recently as Tuesday morning.

We're right to react to suffering and disaster in that way. Jesus warns that it is perverse *not* to sit up and take notice when bad things happen:

> "When you see a cloud rising in the west, immediately you say, 'It's going to rain,' and it does. And when the south wind blows, you say, 'It's going to be hot,' and it is." Luke 12:54–55

We all know how to interpret the weather. And yet, says Jesus, there are some who stubbornly refuse to do the same with world events:

> "Hypocrites! You know how to interpret the appearance of the earth and the sky. How is it that you don't know how to interpret this present time?" Luke 12:56

That stinging reproach prompted some of his listeners to bring up a recent event that had horrified the nation: in an act of terrorism that was religiously motivated, the Roman governor Pontius Pilate had ordered a group of Galilean Jews to be murdered. And, as if to cause maximum outrage and offence, he mingled their blood with the blood of their animal sacrifices.

Some of the crowd bring the incident to Jesus' attention as if to say, "Well, if we're supposed to 'interpret this present time', Jesus, tell us why this atrocity happened!" What exactly is God saying to us through this evil act, and the countless others that have followed it since?

As he answers, Jesus brings up another incident that was just as fresh in the mind. However, this time, it was not the obvious result of human evil. It was one of those unexpected, unforeseen events that seem to occur almost at random. No-one was to blame. It happened in a town called Siloam, where eighteen people had been crushed when a tower collapsed on them. In the aftermath, there must have been people who lamented the fact that that their loved ones were simply in the wrong place at the wrong time. Equally, there would have been those who accidentally side-stepped death simply because they happened to leave for work a little bit later than usual.

So with these two national tragedies in view, what does Jesus say?

> "Do you think that these Galileans were worse sinners than all the other Galileans because they suffered this way? I tell you, no! But unless you repent, you too will all perish." Luke 13:2–3

> "Or those eighteen who died when the tower in Siloam fell on them – do you think they were more guilty than all the others living in Jerusalem? I tell you, no! But unless you repent, you too will all perish." Luke 13:4–5

Notice what Jesus does *not* say. He does not say, "They deserved it." Just a few weeks after the Asian tsunami in late 2004, a Muslim cleric was reported as saying that the disaster affected that particular part of the world because of the rampant immorality in those areas. The drinking and the partying and the "sex tourism" were being judged by Allah, he said. I have also heard some Christians say a similar thing.

In the case of the two tragedies confronting Jesus, he strongly refutes that suggestion: "I tell you, no!" These deaths were not specific punishments meted out by God for particular sins these people had committed. And equally, those who had managed to avoid death were no more virtuous than those who were killed.

In the aftermath of tragedy, the media often talk about "innocent victims". Jesus, shockingly, does not follow suit. Instead, he asks the questions, "Do you think [they] were *worse* sinners...?" and "do you think they were *more* guilty than all the others living in Jerusalem?". His implication is clear: *everyone* living in Jerusalem at that time was guilty of sin. Those who died were not *more* guilty than anyone else, *but they were guilty*, says Jesus, *just as you are*.

As we've seen already in this book, all of us are guilty of rebelling against a God of infinite goodness, holiness and truth. However, his tolerance of our rebellion, and all the suffering it causes, is not infinite. When death comes, we will find ourselves face to face with him, and how many of us are ready for that moment? That's why, when disaster and suffering strike, the right response is to acknowledge the fragility of life, and make sure we are ready to have it taken from us. Because whether it happens on a Tuesday morning in the office, a sun-drenched beach in Thailand, or more predictably on a hospital bed, it will happen.

"Unless you repent, you too will all perish." These are tough words to say to suffering people. But they were spoken by a man who suffered – at the very least – questions over the legitimacy of his birth, racial abuse, betrayal by his friends, alienation from his family, torture, malicious gossip, hunger, thirst, homelessness, religious persecution, the death of a dearly-loved friend, unfair condemnation at a rigged trial, extreme loneliness and an excruciatingly prolonged execution.

He wept – just as we do – when he witnessed suffering. And so great was his compassion that he gave up his own life to do something definitive about it. At the cross, he demonstrated God's desire to forgive each one of us for our wilful rebellion against him. He didn't have to do it, and it was not something we deserved.

If you've picked up this book at a time of great personal suffering, and you doubt God's goodness, look to the cross:

> "For God *so loved the world* that he gave his one and only
> Son, that whoever believes in him shall not perish but have
> eternal life." John 3:16, my italics

At the cross, we see a suffering God, suffering for his own people because he loves them and wants to free them from all suffering in eternity.

All that remains for us to do, as Jesus told the crowd still bewildered by the loss of life at Siloam, is "repent", or to put it another way, "turn back to God." And those words were not spoken by someone seeking to frighten, intimidate or bully. Neither were they spoken by someone who does not know what it means to suffer. In fact, they were spoken by a man shortly to die on your behalf.

11

"Why Do You Hate Sex?"

Sex sells. At the time of writing, sex is selling celebrity gossip magazines, sports utility vehicles and shampoo.

Sex buys, too. Sex is currently buying promotion in the boardroom, power in the bedroom, and pornography in the hotel room.

There are so many tricks we can teach sex: it's a passport, a weapon, a currency, a drug. It's also a commodity. A man recently told me he'd been thinking about the virtues of visiting a prostitute. "After all," he reasoned, "why do you think men take women out for a meal and a movie? It's just a long-winded, hypocritical way of paying for sex. At least my way, you don't pay for a meal you don't want to eat or a movie you don't want to see." If sex is just a commodity to be traded, then I guess he has a point. Why waste all that time in restaurants and movie theatres?

As feminist author Naomi Wolf writes, it's not just men who have been drawn in to the downgrading of sex:

> We've raised a generation of young women…who don't understand sexual ethics like: Don't sleep with a married man; don't sleep with a married woman; don't embarrass people with whom you had a consensual sexual relationship. They don't see sex as sacred or even very important any more. That's been lost. Sex has been commodified and drained of its deeper meaning.[1]

---

[1] Naomi Wolf, *The Washington Post Magazine*, 15 August 2004.

The results of this attitude to sex are not hard to trace in the tragic statistics concerning sexually transmitted diseases, unwanted children and sexual abuse.[2] Buying or selling, it doesn't matter: as Wolf implies, *we like to abuse sex*. If anyone hates sex, it's not God. It's us.

I'll admit this was not an easy chapter to research. For example, there was a moment when a colleague (looking over my shoulder) asked me why two weeks of my calendar had the word "SEX" written repeatedly across it. He looked genuinely concerned, as if he thought I was working too hard.

But the more I read on the subject, the more it became clear that I didn't need to feel self-conscious about sex at all. God doesn't. Far from hating sex, God invented it. *He chose to create it in the first place.* The very first book of the Bible tells us that God created us male and female, with all the physical difference that entails. We read that, "God saw all that he had made, *and it was very good.*"[3]

A little later in the Bible, there's a book called The Song of Solomon. Much of the book is devoted to the subject of sex, and it's not for the faint of heart or the easily embarrassed. The Song of Solomon is a resoundingly passionate celebration of erotic love. And it was written by God. At one point, we read this:

> Eat, O friends, and drink;
>> drink your fill, O lovers.   Song of Solomon 5:1

Two observations: he's not talking about food here, and that doesn't sound much like a God who hates sex.

---

[2] The website of Avert, an international AIDS charity, reports that in the UK, two of the most common sexually transmitted diseases have shown "massive rises" between 1996 and 2005. In one instance, the increase has been a staggering 2,054%.

[3] Genesis 1:31, my italics.

It's also worth noticing that although sex is clearly a means of childbearing (God tells the first human beings to "be fruitful and increase in number"[4]), it's not just about making babies. You will look in vain for a single word about pregnancy in The Song of Solomon. There are, however, hundreds and hundreds of words openly praising the sensual delights of sex and sexual attraction.

OK, but doesn't God want to restrict the way people have sex?

Don't we all? What I mean is: we *all* want to restrict the way people have sex, however liberal we may be. To give one example, very few people think it is acceptable for adults to have sex with young children. So we draw a line there. And most people think it's wrong to have sex with another man's wife. So we draw another line there.

We all draw lines somewhere, the only question is: how do we know we've drawn our lines in the right places? How do we know that *our* views on sex are the right ones? How can we be sure that our views are not just the product of the culture we live in? How can we be sure that our sexual rules really work for the good of everyone?

As the creator of sex, God has something to say about how we use it. God made sex extremely pleasurable, but he also made it extremely powerful. That's why The Song of Solomon warns us three times: "Do not arouse or awaken love until it so desires."[5] Like other powerful things, sex can easily be used in destructive ways, so God doesn't give us the gift without also giving us the loving guidance to go with it.

For a start, God carefully created the context in which sex can be fully protected, appreciated and enjoyed: he

---

[4] Genesis 1:28. [5] Song of Solomon 2:7; 3:5; 8:4.

created marriage, the place where a man and a woman are united physically, spiritually and emotionally.

God's mathematics are strange and beautiful, because when it comes to marriage (and sex for that matter), one plus one equals one:

> ...a man will leave his father and mother and be united to his wife, and they will become one flesh.　　　　Genesis 2:24

Jesus, quoting Genesis, reiterates the same striking equation:

> "'...a man will leave his father and mother and be united to his wife, and the two will become one flesh.' So they are no longer two, but one."　　　　Mark 10:7–8

Marriage – one man and one woman in a loving, lifelong commitment to one another – was created by God and affirmed by Jesus. It is the God-given environment in which sex can be enjoyed to the maximum, while maximising the emotional and spiritual protection of the man and the woman (not to mention children) involved. In fact, sex was deliberately designed by God to deepen the "oneness" of marriage.

Sex joins people together in a way that goes beyond the merely temporary and physical. In some profound, irreversible, God-given way, two become one. It's the reason why paying for sex with a prostitute is never as uncomplicated as exchanging money for a commodity, and saving the unnecessary expense of a meal and a movie. We leave more than money behind us when we get dressed and walk away. "Do you not know," says 1 Corinthians 6 verse 16, "that he who unites himself with a prostitute is one with her in body? For it is said, 'The two will become one flesh.'"

It's also the reason why sex outside marriage causes great harm to the people involved. J. Budziszewski tells the story of a university professor who tried to make this point to his students. Taking a six-inch strip of adhesive tape, he picked on the hairiest student in the room, asking him to roll up his sleeve.

"Now," the professor said, "Tell the tape not to stick." The student obliged: "Don't stick, tape!" The professor pressed the tape down on his forearm and said, "Let's see whether the tape obeys."

With a single rip, he tore the tape off the student's arm. The student yelped.

"Let's try it again," said the professor, as he pressed the tape down in the same place, and pulled it off again. "Any better?"

"A little bit," said the student warily. "How many times are you going to do that, professor?"

"As many as it takes for the tape to obey."

The professor repeated the process five times and each time, of course, the tape was less sticky than the time before.

After the fifth time, the professor said to the student, "Now tell the tape to stick."

He did.

But no matter how hard the professor pressed the tape on the student's arm, it simply fell off again. It just would not stick.

Our sexuality does something similar. The first time we use it, we stick to whoever it touches. However hard we tell it not to stick, sex can't help sticking. That's what it's for. So when we try to tear ourselves loose, it harms us.

Not only that, but when we do get loose, our sexuality is not as "sticky" as it was before. After a while, if it's pulled away from person after person, it just stops sticking.

Sexual partners become more and more like strangers, and we start to feel less and less for the people we're having sex with. The longing for intimacy drives us on, but our capacity to satisfy that longing has been spoiled.

It's not only Christian writers who have noticed this. The novelist Josephine Hart, author of *Damage*, said in an interview: "The idea today is that sleeping around doesn't matter. I'm not making any kind of religious point here, I'm just saying that if you sleep around with enough people you're pretty much on the way to guaranteeing that you'll not recognise profound erotic love when it comes to you. You pay a price for it. I'm not saying it's a moral price [or] that it's a moral issue, [but] you pay a psychological price. And you might just miss it when it happens."[6]

We may be tempted to think, "I'll enjoy sex now, and settle down with someone later." But if we use sex in that way, our very deepest desires for closeness and commitment may well remain unfulfilled.

So you're saying that sex should only happen in marriage, which is a lifelong union between a man and a woman? Isn't that incredibly narrow?

However it may seem at first, it's hard to dismiss Jesus' affirmation of marriage as the product of small-mindedness or cultural naivety. As we've seen, Jesus consistently loved people in a way that even those who don't follow him admire. His words only make sense when we understand that they were spoken to protect us. When we remove these God-set boundaries, ignore the loving creator of sex, and do things our own way – whether it be sex outside marriage, or sexual relations

---

[6] Josephine Hart, interviewed in *The Daily Telegraph*.

between two people of the same sex – there are serious repercussions. The temptation is always to think that we know better, but, as G K Chesterton warns, "Don't ever take a fence down until you know why it was put up."

We are free to live as we please, to take the fences down. But is our way of life really beneficial to us? Does our sexual "freedom" really result in contentment? Or does it just become an even fiercer tyrant than the one we were trying to depose in the first place?

In first century Corinth, people were saying to the biblical writer Paul, "everything is permissible for me" and he answered:

> "Everything is permissible for me" – but not everything is beneficial. "Everything is permissible for me" – but I will not be mastered by anything.   1 Corinthians 6:12

For those whose watchword is "freedom", Paul in effect warns, "Be careful with your freedom. What you do with sex may not be good for you. And be careful that your 'freedom' doesn't become a kind of slavery."

If you think about it, everyone is living for something. Everyone serves a Master. For example, if a person lives for reputation, then they become a slave to what people think. If a person lives for money, then money will call the shots in that person's life, and they become a slave to it. If a person lives for their independence, they become a slave to their desire to avoid commitment. Everyone serves a Master, whether it be reputation, or money, or achievement, or sex, or whatever. The only question is, does your Master have your best interests at heart? *Has he proved that he can give you deep and lasting satisfaction?*

In C. S. Lewis' book *The Screwtape Letters,* even the devil Screwtape knows what we nearly always forget:

that God is out to make people happy. He has made us with the capacity to enjoy far greater pleasures than the ones we usually content ourselves with, if only we will trust the guidance he gives. Even his calls to self-control, self-sacrifice, worship and obedience are just clever ways to help people feel greater and greater pleasure. As Screwtape explains, begrudgingly but truthfully:

> [God is] a hedonist at heart. All those fasts and vigils and stakes and crosses are only a facade. Or only like foam on the sea shore. Out at sea, out in His sea, there is pleasure and more pleasure. He makes no secret of it; at His right hand are "pleasures forevermore"... He has filled the world full of pleasures.

It's important to understand that the boundaries God sets for sex are not there to ruin our sexual pleasure: they have been specifically created to deepen and intensify sex, the way a wide, shallow trickle of water can become a surging, pounding torrent when the riverbank narrows.

When I first tried skiing, I remember my instructor telling me to do all sorts of things that didn't feel natural to me. *Bend your knees, and face down the slope.*

I wanted to stand up and turn *away* from the slope.

But as I began to obey the instructor, something odd happened. I didn't fall over so much. I gained confidence. I got better and better. And the more I did what he said, the better I became. Suddenly I found myself able to race away from the nursery slopes and glide all over the mountain. It's strange but true: obeying the instructor gave me incredible, exhilarating freedom.

That's not to say that my new-found freedom didn't have limits (*stay away from the cliff edges*), but I knew that those limits were there to *increase* my enjoyment, not ruin it.

So as well as creating sex good, God also created good sex. It was given to us, like every gift God gives us, for our enjoyment. When we remove sex from the context he has specifically created for it – because we don't understand (or aren't willing to trust) the goodness of God and the goodness of his intentions toward us – sex is no longer our servant, but our Master. That's why the Bible contains this warning:

> Flee from sexual immorality. All other sins a man commits are outside his body, but he who sins sexually sins against his own body. 1 Corinthians 6:18

Though we may not realise it, if we try to take sex to a place it was never intended to be, we end up hurting ourselves. That's also the loving warning of Proverbs, where God tells us:

> Can a man scoop fire into his lap
> without his clothes being burned?
> Can a man walk on hot coals
> without his feet being scorched? Proverbs 6:27–28

To put it another way, fire in the fireplace is good, but if we take it out of that context, we'll get burned.

And if we're being honest, we must admit that all of us have done exactly that. Jesus said this:

> "You have heard that it was said, 'Do not commit adultery.' But I tell you that anyone who *looks* at a woman lustfully has already committed adultery with her in his heart."
>
> Matthew 5: 27–28, my italics

As Jesus makes clear, even lusting after someone is a serious matter. When it comes to sexual purity, none of us has the right to look down on anyone else because we think *we* have a better record.

But how can God say that sex is only to be enjoyed within lifelong, heterosexual marriage when that seems so far away from the person I am?

Sometimes, we have real trouble accepting that God's intentions towards us *are* good and loving, given the strength of our sexual feelings. But all of us – regardless of our age, sexuality and previous life experience – all of us must measure the reality of God's love for us not by the way we feel, but by the small hill just outside Jerusalem where Christ died. If we start to wonder whether God's intentions towards us are loving, listen to this startling truth: "God demonstrates his own love for us in this: While we were still sinners, Christ died for us."[7]

The cross settles the question of God's love once and for all. Because if you look at the cross, you'll see someone who loved you so much that he actually died for you; someone who loves you more than any sexual relationship can express; someone who, because of his death and resurrection, gives you the power – through his Spirit[8] – to become more and more like him; in short, you'll see someone who wants the very best for you. Instead of asking sex to affirm who you are and fulfil your deepest longings, ask Jesus Christ to do that for you. Trust him when he says: *I have come that you may have life and have it to the full.*[9]

I started by saying that if anyone hates sex, it's not God. It's us.

I think it's also true to say that if anyone values sex highly, it's not us. It's God. No-one celebrates sex more than the creator of sex himself.

But nothing, not even sex, can satisfy like God can.

---

[7] Romans 5:8.
[8] In John 14:15–17, Jesus promises his followers that the Spirit of God will come to live in them, and will help them to obey him.
[9] John 10:10.

12

"Why Don't You Just Do A Miracle?"

"If you are listening, and you are really there, show yourself right now... Do a colossal miracle... Show me something more than ancient hearsay to prove your existence." That's the way Edward Tabash, a Beverley Hills lawyer, addressed God at the University of California. And when there was apparently no response, Tabash concluded that the case was closed.[1]

Similar, though much more gently and thoughtfully expressed, was the sentiment of my neighbour, Bill, who recently asked me, "Why doesn't God just do a miracle, like the ones he did when he was here? Just one miracle would make it so much easier to believe."

Exactly. If he gave us a universal, unmistakable sign of his existence, everyone would believe, wouldn't they?
In his Gospel, John records many of the miracles Jesus did. He tells us about Jesus turning water into wine, healing a man who was terminally ill and telling a man who was "an invalid for thirty-eight years" to get up and walk (which he immediately does). As we read on, we hear of the time Jesus fed more than 5,000 people with five loaves of bread and two small fish. Everyone in the crowd ate "as much as they wanted" and yet, somehow, there were still twelve baskets full of leftovers at the end.

---

[1] Quoted in John Blanchard, *Where Is God When Things Go Wrong?* (Evangelical Press, 2005).

Pushing further into John's Gospel, we read about Jesus walking on water, and giving sight to a man born blind. [2] And then Jesus ups the ante even further. He goes to the tomb of a man who has been dead four days – and gives him back his life.[3]

The man's name is Lazarus.

His sister is wary of removing the stone from his tomb: "by this time there is a bad odour, for he has been there four days." But Jesus insists.

There is no elaborate ritual, no complicated medical procedure, no mysterious ointment is applied. Only three words are spoken: "Lazarus, come out!". And Lazarus emerges, his hands, feet and face still wrapped in the grave clothes he'd been buried in four days previously.

All this takes place in front of a crowd of people ("many Jews had come to Martha and Mary to comfort them in the loss of their brother"). And, as you'd expect, these people told many other people what had happened: "...the crowd that was with him when he called Lazarus from the tomb and raised him from the dead continued to spread the word."[4]

From time to time I hear stories about someone being raised from the dead. The story always emanates from a far-off land and no-one ever seems to have met anyone who actually saw the event. Certainly, no-one ever seems to have met the person who was actually raised from death. But this is very, very different. When Jesus raised Lazarus from the dead, a crowd of people saw it happen. That crowd – and many, many others – met Lazarus afterwards and talked to him about what had happened.

---

[2] These events are recorded in John chapters 2, 4, 5, 6, and 9.

[3] You can find this incident in John 11.

[4] John 12:17.

But not everyone was happy to see Lazarus again. In fact, having only just escaped the clutches of death, some people already want him dead. Again.

> So the chief priests made plans to kill Lazarus as well [as Jesus], for on account of him many of the Jews were going over to Jesus and putting their faith in him.   John 12:10–11

The "chief priests" knew that dead men tell no tales. But unfortunately for them, this one did. And he was telling people that Jesus was the one they should follow, not the chief priests. In effect, Lazarus was living proof of Jesus' divine power. And the chief priests do not like that at all. They know that it will mean an end to the power they've enjoyed for so long.

But surely what you've just said proves my point! This very public miracle caused people to put their trust in Jesus. Why not do the same thing again?

Unfortunately, not everyone *did* put their trust in him, despite the powerful evidence. Even after repeated – and spectacularly public – miracles which could not be explained away even by those who opposed him, this was the response to Jesus:

> Even after Jesus had done all these miraculous signs *in their presence,* they still would not believe in him.
>
> John 12:37, my italics

On first hearing, it sounds incredible, doesn't it? People personally witness miracles performed by a man claiming to be the Son of God, and they walk away unchanged. Again, a matter of hours after Jesus had fed five thousand people with five small loaves and two small fish[5] – a miracle

---

[5] This incident is recorded in John chapter 6.

witnessed by the disciples – we discover that "many of his disciples turned back and no longer followed him."

That being the case, can we be sure that if God were to work a miracle for us now, right in front of our very eyes, we would automatically believe in him?

Not according to Jesus. He insists that miracles in themselves are not enough, because miracles only point us toward a truth that not all of us are willing to accept.

Let me give you an example. After Jesus miraculously feeds five thousand people, he explains what he has done by saying "I am the bread of life", "I am the living bread that came down from heaven" and "he who feeds on this bread will live for ever." In other words, the miraculous provision of food is simply an illustration of a far bigger truth: that Jesus himself is the one who sustains us, that he himself is the one who came down from heaven to offer us eternal life. As it says in the book of Acts: "he himself gives all men life and breath and everything else."[6]

But not everyone who witnesses a miracle can accept the truth it illustrates:

> On hearing it, many of his disciples said, "This is a hard teaching. Who can accept it?" John 6:60

They'd seen the miracle. In fact, the taste of the miracle was still fresh on their tongue. But they still walk away.

Why? For the same reason people walk away now. Not because they lack evidence, but because they don't like the implications of his teaching. They simply aren't willing to submit to God as the one who gives them every breath they draw. They don't trust that he wants what is best for them.

---

[6] Acts 17:25.

It's been 15 years since I first saw this principle working itself out in real life. Remember Steve, from chapter 1? He was a good friend who worked alongside me in the newspaper business for many years. Over that time, as we talked, Steve became convinced not only that God exists, but that Jesus is who he claims to be. We no longer had debates about whether the Bible was trustworthy because Steve was reading it and realising for himself that it is. So convinced was he that I'd walk into the office and find him trying to persuade others that Jesus is God. He'd seen the overwhelming evidence for himself, he no longer tried to deny it, and – more than that – he actively tried to convince others that what he'd discovered was the truth.

But – and I say this with great sadness – Steve never actually became a follower of Christ. He knew it was true, he even stuck his neck out trying to persuade others of the fact, but he never actually walked the walk. Why? Because he knew that if he followed Jesus, he would have to change things in his life. And there were some things he was not prepared to change.

The truth is, Steve did not need a miraculous sign to make him a follower of Christ. He simply needed to trust him.

13

"So, God,

If You Could Ask Me One Question,

What Would It Be?"

Have you heard the one about the rich farmer?

That's not the question God would ask you, by the way – we'll get to that in a moment.

The rich farmer is an entrepreneur who longs to accumulate enough wealth so that he can retire early and enjoy the fruits of his labour. After a particularly impressive crop, the man hatches a plan.

> This is what I'll do. I will tear down my barns and build bigger ones, and there I will store all my grain and my goods. And I'll say to myself, "You have plenty of good things laid up for many years. Take life easy; eat, drink and be merry."
>
> Luke 12:18–19

Sounds good. Being the astute businessman he is, he develops a brilliant business plan, minimising waste and maximising profits. He understands the rules of supply and demand, so he makes sure not to flood the market. He also ensures that his yield will be tax efficient. The plan is a dead certainty because no detail is overlooked. He will have enough money to do whatever he likes, whenever he likes, as often as he likes, and he will never have to do another day's work as long as he lives.

Which, unfortunately, is not very long.

And although the guests at the rich man's retirement party would have slapped him on the back, calling him "a shrewd investor", "a smooth operator", and "a lucky so-and-so", Almighty God has another name for him:

> God said to him, "You *fool!* This very night your life will be demanded from you. Then who will get what you have prepared for yourself?" Luke 12:20, my italics

"This", says Jesus in verse 21, "is how it will be with anyone who stores up things for himself but is not rich toward God."

Although it sounds very careless, losing everything you've ever worked for, everything you've ever wanted, *even losing life itself*, is the easiest thing in the world to do. You simply give it to the wrong person.

In the case of the farmer, that person was himself. Look at the way he speaks: "What shall *I* do? *I* have no place to store *my* crops… This is what *I'll* do. *I* will tear down *my* barns and build bigger ones, and there *I* will store all *my* grain and *my* goods. And *I'll* say to *myself*…" Me, my, I. He's the master of his own destiny, or so he thinks.

But is that the way things really are? According to the man who has confronted us again and again throughout this book, no. According to him, if you *really* want to look after yourself, if you really want to plan for the future, if you really want to save your life, there is only one person you can trust with something so valuable:

"...whoever wants to save his life will lose it, but whoever loses his life *for me* will save it. What good is it for a man to gain the whole world, and yet lose or forfeit his very self?"

Luke 9:24–25, my italics

The farmer "gained the whole world", only to lose it all. But, *if you give your life to me*, says Jesus, *you will save it*. After all that you've read about Jesus, ask yourself if you think he can be trusted. *You can go your own way*, says Jesus, *but please don't. You'll lose the most valuable thing you have.*

So, if I had to guess, here's the one question I think God would ask you: "What good is it if you gain the whole world, and yet lose or forfeit your very self?"

And that's a question only *you* can answer.

What Now?

Good question. Here are some suggestions.

• Talk to God.
It may be that you've become convinced that you can trust Jesus with your life. You know that you've rebelled against God and have not treated other people as you should. But you understand that Jesus willingly died on the cross "as a ransom for many". You want to accept that forgiveness for yourself, and begin an amazing new life following him. If that's you, talk to God about these things.

If you do decide to begin following Jesus, it's a good idea to tell another Christian so that they can support you. And I'd love to know too! Drop me a line here: onequestion@christianityexplored.org.

• Read a Gospel.
You've already read quite a bit about Jesus' life. But the best way of getting to know him is by reading one of the historical accounts of his life: Matthew, Mark, Luke or John. If you don't have one of these "Gospels", write to us and we'll be delighted to send you a free copy: Christianity Explored, c/o All Souls Church, Langham Place, London W1B 3DA.

• Join a Course.
If you'd still like to ask God one question (or several), why not join a Christianity Explored course near you? It's

informal and relaxed. You won't be asked to read aloud, pray or sing. You can ask any question you like, or you can just sit and listen. Visit www.christianityexplored.org and click on "Find a Course".

• **Dig Deeper.**
Other people have written longer books covering these questions – and many others you may have – in much more detail.

If you'd like to dig deeper on a particular question, visit www.christianityexplored.org/onequestion for some recommended reading.

Acknowledgements

If it weren't for the following people, you would have been holding this book months ago. But thankfully, they intervened.

We both want to thank the twelve people who carefully read the first draft and gave us numerous encouragements, suggestions and insights. Our thanks also go to Tim Thornborough for his generous and good-humoured input. (And our apologies to the young man he was sitting opposite on the train who was forced to listen to several chapters before escaping at Bury St. Edmunds).

We would never have been able to complete the task without the warmth, kindness and patience of Caroline Williams. And finally, Sam Shammas. There is barely a paragraph in this book – or in any of the books she has worked on these past six years – that has not been improved by the conscientiousness, care and clarity that she brings to every project. We are so grateful to God for her.

Paul Williams and Barry Cooper
September 2007